THE *Single* HEART

THE *Single* HEART

Langré Edwards

WESTBOW
PRESS®
A DIVISION OF THOMAS NELSON
& ZONDERVAN

WestBow Press books may be ordered through booksellers or by contacting:

WestBow Press
A Division of Thomas Nelson & Zondervan
1663 Liberty Drive
Bloomington, IN 47403
www.westbowpress.com
1 (866) 928-1240

ISBN: 978-1-9736-5528-2 (sc)
ISBN: 978-1-9736-5529-9 (hc)
ISBN: 978-1-9736-5527-5 (e)

Library of Congress Control Number: 2019902801

Print information available on the last page.

WestBow Press rev. date: 03/28/2019

To my readers

Gold and treasure have been placed within each of you. I pray that as you read this book, your hearts are set ablaze with a desire for wholeness and that you experience the undeniable, never-ending, always-pursuing, overwhelming love of God (Romans 8:31–39).

To my mom

You continuously planted many seeds of wisdom in me that make up much of the "fruit" written within this book. Your life of endurance, resilience, and grace has inspired me every day.

To my ministry family

You prayed and supported me through not only this writing journey but the entirety of my process in itself. You exemplified what it means to be the body of Christ and expressed unconditional love. I couldn't have done this without you.

Contents

Introduction

*I will give you a new heart and put a new
spirit in you; I will remove from you your
heart of stone and give you a heart of flesh.*
—EZEKIEL 36:26 (NIV, EMPHASIS ADDED)

The heart is the central part of our physical and spiritual being. It is a muscle, located a little to the left of the middle of our chests, about the size of a fist. The heart is unique because of what it does. It contains a network of blood vessels that carry blood to and from all areas of our body. This blood provides the rest of the body with the oxygen and nutrients it needs. It's like a pump.

Place your hand on your chest. Do you feel that heartbeat? Your heart is working all day and all night to keep you alive. It never stops. Even though it's working on the inside, how cool is it to know that you can feel it on the outside by checking your pulse? The way we have been designed is truly remarkable!

In our society, we often use figures of speech such as "a heart made of stone," "a broken heart," "listen to your heart," "to break one's heart," and "give your heart to somebody". In various forms of literature, the heart is often referred to as the "seat of emotions," responsible for our ability to exercise compassion, understanding, affection, and intellect. It has been represented as the makeup of our souls (our minds, wills, and emotions). By these phrases, people often imply that the mind, will, and emotions are intricately involved in the descriptions of their heart experiences.

As long as you are alive, you have this muscle working within you to pump the blood and oxygen needed to survive on earth. This organ was so intricately and purposefully crafted. You and I each have a single beating heart that carries us through life. Even more complex is that you and I are unequivocally composed of many different thoughts, feelings, emotions, and desires. The heart is beautiful in all of its arrangements and analogies.

Biblically, why then, would the verse in Ezekiel 36:26 in the opening of this chapter imply that we need a new heart? What's wrong with our hearts? What kind of heart dis-ease is it talking about? How would our hearts become hardened to the point that we required a heart of flesh—something soft, tender? Why would young, healthy, and vibrant people be confronted with the need for a "heart transplant"?

Hello Bermuda

I recall sitting on my bed in my quaint studio apartment, reading this passage of scripture for the first time. It was in 2011, when I moved back to my mother's native land for an employment opportunity, carrying only, as I like to say, "two dollars and a big dream". Although I had lived on my own at university, this was my first major independent and "adult" move. At twenty-two years of age, I felt very far from being an adult and couldn't quite wear that title yet. Bills, a career, credit scores, taxes, and buying my own transportation were so far from my mind that I thought that growing up was ... for grown-ups. Yet, there I was—me, a mattress on the floor, and a few pieces of furniture that had been donated by a friend to get me going in my brand new turnkey and very first "pay your rent on time or get evicted" apartment.

Bermuda, a gorgeous island with pristine pink-sand beaches, was much livelier in the summer months when all the college students were home, with boating, spending the day by the water, and concert events. In the winter everything tended to quiet down so there wasn't a lot to do for entertainment or a variety of events. I spent a lot of time observing my new surroundings, adjusting to the slower paced island life, and equal amount of time in the quiet of no cable and no internet.

In the evenings, after returning from my new job, I was confronted with a time of reflection. I would think about and question my former partying and workaholic city lifestyle. I had been a waiter's assistant (busgirl) and hostess at the Cheesecake Factory, a saleswoman at Kay Jewelers, photographer as a side hustle, and promo girl for some of the hottest clubs in Atlanta. I was always on the go, which didn't grant me much time to reflect on the direction of my life at that point because I never slowed down long enough to do so.

I had moved to Bermuda for one reason only—to make money. I had a plan. The goal was to work for two years and then move to Barcelona, Spain, to become an au pair. I knew that Bermuda, at only twenty-one square miles in size, was too small for my bigger-city mentality. I felt that if I didn't have an escape plan, I would get sucked into the Devil's Triangle with the sea creatures. I didn't want to be in one place for very long. I equated stillness with idleness.

Silence and motionlessness were foreign concepts to me. I felt like I'd moved from a hustle and bustle city life to a desolate and isolated wilderness because I was so far away from family, friends and in a blank canvas of a 350 sq. ft apartment. Yet there I was ... alone with no material comfort and no immediate family nearby. It was an uncomfortable transition period and a total shift.

During this time of frustration, I often whispered to myself, "There's got to be more to life than this." Deep down, I knew I wasn't satisfied. While living in Atlanta and traveling all over, I was exposed to many things. I couldn't believe that all there was to life was the wealth and fame I had seen. My perspective-bubble had been popped, as I saw firsthand the unhappiness that followed sole pursuit of money, power, and fame. I was in a very shallow circle living in the city. I was in the environment and in the company of what had an allure of joy, pleasure, and satisfaction, yet beyond the lust of the eyes, the desire of the flesh, and the pride, they were superficial and unfulfilling. It was like an oasis; it drew me in, but was only an illusion once getting closer. I saw famous celebrities needing more drugs, longer nights of partying, more praise, and more sex to feel powerful. I saw girls pimping themselves between multiple people just to feel wanted and desired; craving attention and thirsting for any kind of affection. I realized that many of the people surrounding me in the club were looking at the bottom of a bottle, trying to drown out their sorrows so they wouldn't sink under their many cares. I listened to my friends in corporate America on the brink of burnout trying to prove their worth and value by the letters behind their name or the number of zeros in their bank account. So much of the world I had idolized as a child about my future started to become vanity and chasing after the wind. I found myself trying to obtain more things and move faster thinking it would cause me to avoid the crushing disappointment I felt when I considered that everything around me might have been smoke and mirrors.

As I sat, day after day, no longer finding happiness from being in my circle of friends, no longer desiring what the others around me still wanted (success and recognition), and struggling with the concept of climbing a ladder, totally unsure of who I was and where I wanted to go, I felt I had only one direction that I had not tried—a real and authentic relationship with God.

> **The Lord is *near to the brokenhearted* and saves the crushed in spirit. (Psalm 34:18, emphasis mine)**

My relationship with the church, religion, and scripture had been one of condemnation, guilt, boring routine, and tons of hypocrisy. My experience was that if I was on the outside of a particular belief, I was the enemy—God didn't love me, and hell was my destination - it came from such a hateful, angry, uptight, joyless, and strictly religious voice. So there was nothing about what I'd experienced, heard, or seen that enticed me to join a religion. As a matter of fact, much of it kept me running as far away as possible.

I didn't know what a relationship with God looked like. I didn't even know what that meant. I didn't really want God because he had allowed my dad to die when I was eleven years old. My dad had been a devout believer, a praying man, a minister of faith, a worship leader. So if God couldn't save him from dying of cancer, what benefit would he be to my life? How "real" could he be?

Having a new thought process to "try God" was a shock, even to me. There was nothing about my lifestyle that said I was ready to get right with God. I'd thought it would be something I'd do when I got old and needed to take my grandbabies to Sunday school but not at age twenty-two. I didn't have anyone around me—certainly not in my circle of friends—who encouraged this thought. In fact, when I talked about learning more about the Bible and *maybe* going to church to check it out, my friends laughed at me.

Was I tripping? Was the move to Bermuda, too much time in silence, or the discomfort my bedding being on the damp floor getting to me?

Something was happening to me. Something felt different. Something (or someone) was tugging on me to go in that direction. I didn't know what it meant, but I did know this: I was tired; exhausted actually. I felt lost. I felt lonely. I had a stone heart of bitterness. I had a broken heart of pain and disappointment. My heart was desperately sick with comparison and never feeling enough. And I was fed up with continuing with the way that things were.

Draw near to God, and he will draw near to you. Cleanse your hands, you sinners, and purify your hearts, you double-minded. (James 4:8, emphasis mine)

Three months after moving, I made a decision. I accepted Jesus as my Lord and Savior after befriending a coworker at my job. From the time I met her, I knew there was something different about her. She was peaceful, and I wanted that peace. I asked her how was it that her demeanor was so calm and peaceful, especially in moments of total chaos in the office. Her speech was different. When I was around her, telling her about my weekends of debauchery and using my extended vocabulary (cursing like a sailor), without her saying a word, I felt this inner conviction within me. The more we talked, she began to share her faith and her testimony with me of how Jesus Christ had transformed her life. For me, it was another tug. Something was in me saying, "this is what you have been searching for." I was already in the process of opening up to the idea that God was "something" I should incorporate into my life, but with the many different religions, I wasn't sure if I should try Buddhism, Christianity, Islam, Hinduism, or Judaism. I adamantly resolved that if God were real, he would have to lead me in the way that I should go. A short few weeks later, after gaining some insight on the true nature of God and mankind's rebellion against Him, I made the confession that I indeed knew that I was a sinner and in total need of a Savior. I understood that God is holy – morally spotless and undefiled, exalted or worthy of complete devotion as one perfect in goodness and righteousness – and with a quick scan of my life, it was apparent I am not. So with that understanding, I could see that we had been enemies. The way I was living was the polar opposite to His very nature. He is Light, and yet my life showed that I loved living in moral darkness. According to His principles, His judgment for me was death. That's what my life was... not a quick or swift death, a slow painful path towards total destruction and death. This actually really grieved me to think about.

But, then I heard the good news that God did not desire for me to remain His enemy, living a life separate from Him, the Source of Life. He had a plan. Instead of me depending on my own righteousness – or lack of it – I could lean on the righteousness of someone else. Jesus Christ.

Jesus is the only one who lived a life of perfect obedience to God, perfect righteousness, not for His own wellbeing, but for you and me. He paid the penalty of our sin by dying for us. Every single lash He took to his body, the crown of thorns shoved into His head, the nails driven into His hands and feet, were really for each one of our sins; past, present, future, known and unknown. He shed his innocent blood and sacrificed His life so that I wouldn't have to. So, how could I knowing this live a life rejecting the one who did this for me?

I began to weep, but it was because I was overwhelmed by this love. No one had ever laid down their life for me like this. It was like a movie scene being played out where right as a bullet is heading toward me, someone decided to jumped in front of it and die in my place. No one had ever expressed such love for me. And yet, before He even knew me, Jesus decided that he would stand in the gap.

I learned that Jesus died on that cross and was buried in a

tomb, but on the third day, something miraculous happened. Jesus was raised to life again. He was victorious over sin and death. This was significate to me because where I felt the separation from God, how I had was so burdened with shame and I identified all of my sinfulness, this gave me a hope that I could be resurrected to new life. I could be transformed too. It promised me rejuvenation and new life. I received it by faith even though I couldn't humanly see it and a hope despite not humanly feeling it. Somewhere within me, I just believed that this was the only thing that could truly reform the human heart. I decided that if I was foolish for having faith in Jesus Christ, I would rather try and give it my all than to live a life of unbelief and at the end of my days find out I was wrong.

I approached my coworker and asked her if she would baptize me.

Bermuda is known for its beautiful aqua-blue waters and pink-sand beaches. On August 12, 2011, I was dunked underwater as a sign of being buried to the old nature and then brought out of the water as a symbol of being washed and made a new person. No hymns were sung, and there was no congregation to whom I turned around to. There was no denomination to which I adhered. There was only a brief moment on a quiet beach, where I sat wondering what this act actually meant to me and my life. I didn't feel different. The heavens didn't open up before me. I didn't see angels and the crowd go wild, but I did hear a small voice speak to my mind: *"You can no longer ignore my Spirit, for now my Spirit is within you."*

That was the first time I heard the voice of God and knew that he was very, *very* real.

For you created my inmost being; you knit me together in my mother's womb. I praise you because I am fearfully and wonderfully made; your works are wonderful, I know that full well. My frame was not hidden from you when I was made in the secret place when I was woven together in the depths of the earth. Your eyes saw my unformed body; all the days ordained for me were written in your book before one of them came to be. How precious to me are your thoughts, God! How vast is the sum of them! Were I to count them, they would outnumber the grains of sand—when I awake, I am still with you.

—PSALM 139:13–18 (NIV)

Chapter 1

A Deceitful Heart

The heart is deceitful above all things, and
desperately wicked; Who can know it? I,
the Lord, search the heart, I test the mind,
even to give every man according to his
ways, according to the fruit of his doings.
—ISAIAH 17:9–10

Over the course of the next seven years, upon asking God to come into my heart—and into my mind, my will, my emotions, and even my physical well-being—I was on a transformative journey. From the first day, unknowingly, I had stepped into my wilderness season. I call it that because a wilderness is an uncultivated, neglected or abandoned region. Like a wilderness, I too was in my wild and still fairly empty state. I knew I was saved, and I believed in Jesus and that he had died for my sins, but I still had all the same junk and gunk going on in my life. This was only the beginning and it was going to require some purging of the old nature, norms and appetites until I was empty enough to be filled up with the new ideas, values, and mindsets.

I was still smoking marijuana and battling to think straight. I read about Jesus being born in a manger and could relate because I was *still* sleeping on a mattress on the floor. I was in the club on Saturday, but at the altar on Sunday, trying to straddle both fences. I was still hanging out with my same friends, doing the same things. I have to admit that it was very hard to live a life of hypocrisy. There wasn't a Friday night out with a glass of wine in my hand that I didn't feel the conviction of God saying, "you don't belong here anymore". I could no longer ignore God's Spirit, but I wasn't entirely clear on what it meant to now have his Spirit living inside me. The difference was that my desires were changing and the tug-o-war I felt on the inside was prompting me to make some decisions.

On my bookshelf sat a pink Bible, engraved with my name, that my parents had given me when I turned ten years old. This Bible was always packed in my boxes whenever I moved. It had great sentimental value and it moved from state to state and across other countries with me. Yet, I never actually opened up its pages. It looked like it had survived a flood, which it did when our basement experienced a ruptured water pipe and submerged our downstairs. It was in one of the boxes in a closet, closest to the overflow. Shockingly, it remained fairly intact despite the binding becoming slightly weathered. It had that old book smell; like moth balls and a sweet mustiness that lingers on worn sheets of paper. The kind of smell that you'd expect one to have when it's been collecting dust on a shelf. This Bible was unique to me because it had my dad's handwriting. My dad wrote in the most fine-looking cursive font and had an eloquence in communicating with the written word. Even today, seeing his handwritten love letters to my mom still melts my heart. Growing up, he could be found writing front and back on a yellow legal sized notepad with a gold cased, fine tipped, ink pen. It is one of my favorite childhood memories of him.

As I reached for the Bible, I experienced such nostalgia and a flood of these precious moments. On the first page, an inscription from him read: "May this Bible guide you your whole life through. May you turn to it when you don't know what to do. For in it is love and wisdom to guide. When you open it up, you're letting God inside."

For some reason, this time when I took it off my shelf and read those words, they seemed bolder, more instructional, and more indicative of the time and space that I was in. I wondered how my father had been inspired to write a poem with guidance and of encouragement. *Is there any benefit in reading this book?* I asked myself. I began to dive into it, reading through first the book of John in the Gospels and then working my way through others.

> For the word of God is living and active, sharper than any two-edged sword, piercing to the division of soul and of spirit, of joints and of marrow, and discerning the thoughts and intentions of the heart. (Hebrews 4:12)

Living. Active. Piercing. Discerning—these words are the Word of God.

As I combed through so many chapters, my mind genuinely was enthralled. I noticed that scripture I had heard quoted had been taken out of context. The ways in which I was living my life were not encouraged and contradicted God's expressed perfect will. One particular scripture caught my attention: "Flee from sexual immorality" (1 Corinthians 6:18). I recall saying uttering aloud, "Wait! You want me to run from sex with my boyfriend?" I felt I was being challenged and corrected, yet made to fall in love all at the same time. My head was spinning with glee and excitement because this was a breath of fresh air. It was opposite of what people using scriptures to control, manipulate, and dominate had made me feel. It refreshed my hope because it gave me new perspective. I couldn't believe that what I was reading was the polar opposite of the direction I was going. It gave me whiplash—in the best way. My jaw was always on the floor as I spent hours and hours highlighting passages and writing in my journal.

Being a novice to reading the Bible, Jesus, and these new commands, I didn't fully understand prayer. *What was it? Why do we do it? What's the purpose?* I pondered. I had vaguely prayed in the past by calling on God in times of turmoil and distress, but not much changed, and probably because I asked with no intention to make the appropriate changes to get out of my mess. As a result, I clearly had deceived myself into thinking he wasn't interested in my prayers. I often felt like my prayers were merely words that went out, hit the ceiling, and bounced back. I didn't actually think that prayers "worked." But as I studied more, I knew that prayer would need to become a by-product of my newfound faith. I learned there were things in my life, such as a lack of faith and unconfessed sin, that blocked my prayers. My issue wasn't a God-problem; it was a me problem. I needed to allow some things in my life to change if I was going to have the correct heart motive and even the room to receive what I was asking for. I eventually picked up a book called *The Purpose and Power of Prayer* by Dr. Myles Monroe, which gave me more understanding. But, at the time I settled for just speaking aloud, and with my tiny pea sized childlike faith, I believed God would hear me. After all, He brought me to this point anyways. So, I began to simply talk to God about what I was reading and how it made me feel, and I asked why my reality was parallel to the words of Jesus.

One evening I heard a small voice encouraging me to look up two scriptures. The first one would be an answer to my prayer for God to show me my current heart issues: "The heart is deceitful above all things, and desperately sick; who can understand it?" (Jeremiah 17:9).

As things stood, based on measuring myself against others, I believed that I was a kind and righteous person. I didn't judge myself by any criteria, only by what everyone else typically thinks about himself or herself. I didn't murder anyone like Adolf Hitler. I wasn't seeking to do wicked toward people, as Pol Pot had, by creating a mass genocide, as had the Khmer Rouge. I sometimes gave money to the homeless, which could have shown Mother Teresa–like characteristics. I had done a ton of community service hours back in high school, and I technically wasn't struggling-struggling, as compared to a lot of people in the world. In my mind, I could always find something to rationalize with to make me feel righteous. Things weren't great, but they could have been worse. So why would I complain?

What Makes Our Hearts Deceitful?

Our hearts become deceitful when we forget that, in our corrupt and fallen sin state, we operate falsely. The heart of humankind, when in this position, will almost always lean toward calling evil good and good evil—putting false colors on things. Mankind has a knack for taking something beautiful, pure, honorable and lovely and completely distorting or perverting its purpose. Consciously or subconsciously we natural drift. God knows this about us, even if we haven't accepted this about us.

I, the Lord, search the heart …

None of us knows what is completely in our hearts or another person's heart; it is unsearchable to us. God, however, is all-knowing. He is perfectly acquainted with our hearts and everything that lodges within them—all the thoughts, counsels, and desires yet secret. All our hearts' intentions, affections, and determinations are in the light before him. Even though we can successfully hide them before everyone else, we will always be fully known and seen in totality before God.

The way that God will reveal what's in us is almost always through a test or a trial. You won't know that you struggle with a quick temper until you have someone cut you off in traffic. You don't realize the depth of your levels to procrastinate until given a swift deadline. You will justify worry and anxiety when you are confronted with the offer of cast those cares. You won't understand that you idolize something until you are prompted to give it up. God's work of creating new hearts within us comes by our first asking him to do so, and then he begins to exam our hearts to show us what is within them. It's usually not the most comfortable process. However, as we agree with him that we are desperately in need of his help, he fills our hearts with new ideas, new wisdom, and new desires. He indeed takes out the heart of stone and gives us a heart of flesh, tender and receptive to his will. God did a work in me, and I believe that he wants to do a work in you too, perhaps through a related process and through this book.

In reading the verse in Jeremiah 17:9 about the deceitfulness of our hearts and while thinking over my life, I came to realize I had no standard against which to hold myself. My measure of good and evil was all over the map. My perception was that I was a good person who occasionally did bad things. It was evident that my highway to hell was paved with good intentions, as the expression goes. As I kept reading, studying, and praying, however, I realized that when measured against God's standard for purity, righteousness, and holiness, I was *far* from it. I submit that most of us think we are good, but we are wrong. There is evidence in all our lives that it is human nature to pursue evil, whether it's tax dodging or gossiping at church, whether we're the lustful liar or the serial murderer. I saw my own wickedness and mishandling of my freedom of choice honestly, transparently, and humbly. It made me realize that although I was not physically sick, I had a massive problem with the condition of my soul. I was spiritually bankrupt and morally deficient.

At that moment, I began to repent. I felt extreme remorse for the way I had been living my life. I had lived entirely as God's enemy and adversary because I lived in contradiction to his will and ways. I was ashamed for the times I had gossiped about other girls' personal business. I regretted having given my body to boyfriends who never intended to make a commitment beyond the physical. I saw the error of living so selfishly in self-ambition, self-exaltation, and self-service. And I lamented because I could not believe that God had sent his Son to die on the cross for these sins so that I could receive forgiveness and a new life and be accepted—no longer his enemy but now a daughter, his beloved, a friend, and a vessel for his use. *Oh, what kind of love is this?*

We Need Purified Hearts

> Create in me a clean heart, O God, and renew a right spirit within me. (Psalm 51:10)

Why do we need to ask God for a clean heart? Why do I need a pure heart? Why do you and I need to allow God to come in and purify our hearts? These were the questions I pondered. I found my answer in the Gospel according to Matthew:

> But what happens out of the mouth proceeds from the heart, and this defiles a person. For out of the heart come evil thoughts, murder, adultery, sexual immorality, theft, false witness, slander. These are what defile a person. But to eat with unwashed hands does not defile anyone. (Matthew 15:18–20)

I saw these things produced in my life. If I wasn't living it out in action, I evidently was meditating on these things in my thought life. Nobody around me would have known the depths of my wrong thinking, yet an omniscient God did. It scared me to think that I could be walking through life in a completely wrong direction. I prayed that if this was true—that what I was holding within my heart was destroying me from the inside out—that God would help me to do an about-face. This scripture was the beginning of my new desire; a desire for purity. Any part of my life that compromised that possibility had to go. I didn't know how my heart had become filled by these things, and I didn't know how to get it back to a right and full condition, but I believed that God could do the impossible.

Purity is defined as being not mixed or adulterated with any other substance of material; free of contamination; wholesome and untainted by immorality, especially that of a sexual nature; clean, clear, and refreshing. However, life had mixed into my soul bitterness, anger, resentment, abandonment, rejection, and the like. I was contaminated with warped thinking, addicted to unhealthy patterns, and in pursuit of continuing in dysfunctional cycles.

The Lord began to show me that I was fragmented. In the area of relationships, the wear and tear of dating without direction had been exhausting and left me feeling the consequences of moving into intimate relationships prematurely and without any qualifiers. When it came to my identity, I had given my heart in pieces to things and people who did not respect it, protect it, or care for it in a way that esteemed me, edified me, and truly reflected the heart of the Father. My heart had learned to do gymnastics through love, loss, hurt, betrayal, and grief. There was a part of me that started to become very cold and detached in my perspective of relationships. I, ashamedly, started to allow bitterness to open me up to believing the damaging mindsets about relationships that are perpetuated in our society. Perspectives like, "all men will cheat" or "you can't trust anybody". This particular toxic direction of thinking led me to take a sabbatical from dating, as I called it, 'a man-fast'. Otherwise, my continuing to date with all of this residue was only me operating broken and perpetuating more brokenness along the way; therefore, God's new Spirit within me revealed to my mind that now I was single, but my heart was still fragmented and divided.

I did not know how twisted my reality had become, how much of *me* I was missing, or how genuine my unquenchable thirst for love, acceptance, and belonging was. I recognized that I may have become my worst enemy by not giving myself the chance to look soberly over my life. By the time I surrendered to following Jesus, I was up to my eyeballs in failed attempts at finding the happiness and intimacy I craved, yet I saw the promise of an internal peace that would surpass my external circumstances.

Ultimately, like Drano to a clogged pipe, there is a process that precedes progress.

Single, But Not Undivided

Above all else, guard your heart, *for everything you do flows from it.* (Proverbs 4:23 NIV, emphasis mine)

Everything in your life flows from what is within you. That's why if you are a divided or incomplete person, you must take notice of this issue. I'd like to define these terms and familiarize you with the idea that every individual on earth should seek to be single. This is not, by any means, an encouragement for those who are married to divorce their spouses. Singleness, in this context, means singleness of mind, heart, and focus as a result of wholeness. It means taking the responsibility to seek to become a complete and healthy person so you can become a part of the solution of healing your family, generations after, communities… and not an addition to the problem.

Throughout this book, I will use terms like *fragmented, whole,* and *single* almost interchangeably.

- fragment—a small part broken off or detached. An incomplete or isolated portion. Divided and broken into pieces.

To be fragmented is the opposite of being whole.

- whole—containing all components; complete. Not wounded, injured or impaired. Sound or unhurt. Having been restored; healed. A thing entire in itself.

To be whole is the true definition of becoming single.

- single—not accompanied by another or others. Not divided; unbroken.

Admittedly, we often relate to the word *single* from a relational standpoint. You might limit this word to meaning "not married" or "not involved in a romantic relationship." It might be an option offered to you on Facebook or a dating website or an option you tick on a form. However, I want to impress on you, whether you are without a partner, dating, married, or divorced, that *becoming single* and maintaining a *single heart* should be your highest and most earnest aim.

Based on these definitions, we will proceed with the notion that regardless of relational status, socioeconomic position, or health, every person should seek becoming single. In other words, you can be single or married but still not a whole person. You can climb the career ladder and still remain a fragmented person. You can be strong and healthy in your body but still not be undivided, restored, and complete within your soul. It is possible to be single but not to be a single individual.

You can *be* and *do* many things while still functioning in a fragmented soulish state. Simply put, our soul-life is our self-life. Our souls are composed of our minds, wills (desires/motives), and emotions, and these are areas that can be wholly compounded with all kinds of wrong thoughts, distorted motivations, and deep roots of dysfunction. It is evident that people can be fully alive while successfully living beneath a mask. A Christian can become soulish when they are not submitted to the Holy Spirit. They can become the "grumblers, complainers, walking according to their own lusts… sensual [soulish] persons, who cause divisions, not having the Spirit" that Jude 16, 19 talks about. Our souls are in need of saving because we live in a world that is fixed on making them into cold, hard, and heartless.

Have you been alive physically but wholly disconnected and disengaged in your everyday life? Is it possible to function in your relationships, day in and day out, without acknowledging a broken connection, a detachment? Does it strike you (as it has me) that there is something terribly wrong with a passionless, passive, mundane, monotonous life? Are you not vaguely unsettled by the idea that somehow your outlook on everything—from God, to relationships with others, to even yourself can end up with the flavor of stale bread?

I began this journey of learning how to move from a guilt-stricken, heartbroken, and confused young girl to becoming a whole woman with a single heart unto the Lord. It took almost seven years before this book was ready to be written. I state the time frame so you realize this is *not* an overnight transformation. As with anything, it takes time. My life has been a tried, tested, and rewarding road that I still walk day by day—and I suspect yours has as well. Wholeness is not limited. It's for us all and offered to us daily through the one named Jesus Christ.

I invite you to walk with me on a journey through brokenness, redemption, restoration, and healing. My hope is that as you read through this book you may understand that nobody is too far away to be restored. No one is too messed up for God to heal. For anyone who has felt defeated in life, I hope this book inspires you to not give up and to believe in change and transformation. I hope it spurs you on to begin a relationship with God so there might be a joy and refreshment for life given to you. If you continue to walk by faith and trust God, I am a witness that he will make everything beautiful with time (Ecclesiastes 3:11).

Welcome to the journey toward a single heart.

Chapter 2

Right Thinking

As a man thinketh, *so he is*.
—PROVERBS 23:7 (EMPHASIS ADDED)

*W*hat we think about, we ultimately become. What we think about determines the course we will take in life. What we hold within our hearts and lock into our focus eventually is spoken from our mouths. Out of the abundance of the heart, the mouth speaks (Luke 6:45). If you are full of darkness, your speech will reveal it. If you are full of light, you will speak life into the people, things, and situations around you. If this is so—and a glimpse of our lives bears evidence of this—then whatever we meditate on is far more important than we may like to believe. Our thoughts can point us in the direction of success, joy, thankfulness, and well-being or the course of depression, depletion, bitterness, and defeat.

Every single day our mind and thoughts are being shaped by the things we are ingesting. The news cultivates ideas about political parties and global issues. Music can get us to sway to a particular messaging. Conversations and dialogues can develop our opinions. We are undoubtedly since day one being molded in our intelligence. But, do we ever truly consider about what we're thinking about?

There is a popular argument today that says human beings do not use their entire brain capacity. This is known as the "10 percent myth." It was best displayed in the Luc Besson movie *Lucy*, starring Scarlett Johansson. Johansson's character is given a drug that causes her to access 100 percent of her brain capacity. It is a theme also seen in TV shows like *Heroes*, in which only a few people possess superhuman abilities, or the movie *Limitless*, with Bradley Cooper when his character Eddie Morra receives a nootropic drug that causes him to have perfect recollection of everything he has ever read and the aptitude to redefined his interpersonal skills. This 10 percent myth could be appealing if you look at it in regard to human potential.

It's one of the reasons why the self-help industry generates close to eleven billion dollars per year. People are looking for ways to build their self-esteem, become smarter, get rich, lose weight, meet their soul mates, be in better shape, and enjoy their lives more. Additionally, it implies that we need more information, more knowledge, more seminars, and drugs to have more, but I propose that we need to debunk the lie the makes us think we are in such great lack. When we believe we lack something, we spend a lot of money, time, and energy trying to find that thing. But the truth is, we can expand our minds, and we can increase our intelligence; it all comes down to how we choose to use our brains. There is a quote by Galileo Galilei that says, "We cannot teach people anything; we can only help them discover it within themselves." We have more power and ability to use our minds for beneficial things, but I would like to suggest that many of us are mismanaging our thought-lives. When we think rightly, our actions will align and point us in the right direction. From the beginning and in our original nature, we were given the power to function with a sound mind (2 Timothy 1:7).

At some point we all may believe that we could achieve more if we applied ourselves, which is not necessarily false. Change, however, is difficult to accomplish. Environmental factors play a role. Habits are deep-seated and stubbornly resistant to the efforts to replace them. Familiar friends and family may feel comfortable with the "old" you and may be reluctant to let go of their impressions of you. I can't even count how many times I have tried to stir myself into a changed attitude, a new year's resolution, diet, or habit with only a short burst of success and frustration to follow. So, much of the change we see could be because of temporary behavior modification, as opposed to a long-term transformation.

The Science of Thoughts

In her book *Switch on Your Brain*, cognitive neurologist Dr. Caroline Leaf delves into the science of thought. She discusses how we can change our brains by becoming aware of our thoughts. Our minds and our brains are different things, but the brain needs the mind, and they work intricately together; the mind works through the brain. The mind is our cognitive awareness. All day long, the mind sends signals to the brain and activates the brain to dispatch information to the rest of the body.

Fun fact: Did you know that you can influence your genetics by the way you think? This is phenomenal because it shows that we can influence how the brain is structured and how it works, as well as the quality of our cells, which can influence the quality of our health. Our bodies are made up of thirty to forty trillion cells, with about two hundred different types of cells—I would say that is a lot of responsibility for our minds/thoughts to impact and affect. Imagine being able to change the genetic make up for your children's children because you improved your thought life!

More than knowing what you do, I would like to see how you think. How do your thoughts show up in your life?

How Do You Think?

Well-known scientist Dr. Marian Diamond came up with the "magic trees of the mind" analogy, which is that our thoughts look like trees. Thus, good thoughts look like a full and flourishing canopy. Negative, toxic thoughts look like wiry, scrawny, and fragile trees. Every time we think what we think, we change the structure of our brains. Every experience we have changes the trees in our brains. Our memories are thoughts; they are stored in these trees, and they continually change. Every day, our experiences, listening to people, and thinking are "gardening" our minds and structuring our brains.

Let's say you have suppressed a toxic memory. You may be able to push that memory far down into the ground, but it can become a root that shows up somewhere down the line. Take the person, for example, who reserves their feelings, doesn't speak up, and continues to hold things in. This method may work for a while, but this person usually detonates overtime if the root issue is not addressed. Or consider the person who has a quick temper because of the root of hurt and now has thick branches of self-preservation and an electric fence around its tree trunk. It may cost them quality relationships and the ability to form healthy connections with others. We must resist the temptation to allow negativity to fester in our lives.

It takes more, however, than the practice of positive thinking and self-will, as you may know from experience. It takes more than just hearing a message about changing your thoughts. And it requires more than merely being aware of your "stinking thinking." It's more than temporary behavior modification. Right thinking comes from acknowledging your wrong thinking, confessing it, understanding that "someone" can help you and go to the root of where that thought process entered; then it can be replaced with a renewed and right perspective that results in true long-term transformation. This is a task for our own personal cognitive neurologist, Jesus Christ.

> *Let this mind be in you*, which was also in Christ Jesus. (Philippians 2:5 KJV, emphasis added)

For me to gain fresh insight and perspective to write this chapter, I needed to renew my mind in areas as well. This chapter was one of the most challenging to write. Everything bombarded my mind with wrong thinking about myself, about finishing this chapter, and about completing this book. However, I professed over and over that what the enemy used to stop me, God worked out for my benefit and gave an opportunity for me to sharpen my practice of learning the power of right thinking and pushed me to studying more on this area.

What Is the Condition of Your Mind?

Have you ever felt like you were losing your mind? No? Well, hang in here for those of us who have.

It may have seemed like the more you wanted to think good and positive thoughts, the more you battled with your thoughts throughout the day. At one point, I felt like the greatest enemy and biggest battle I was facing was the warfare taking place in my own head.

My mind felt perpetually geared toward the negative, the evil, the confused, the anxious, the critical, and the judgmental. My mind felt like it was being attacked by fiery arrows that had been sent to strike my mind. One day, while expressing this ongoing battle to a friend, she reminded me that it is with our minds that we serve the Lord. We're told in the commandment to "Love the Lord your God with all your heart and with all your soul and with all your strength and *with all your mind*" (Luke 10:27, emphasis added). If I was to honor God with my intellect and clear thinking, I needed to accept the fact my reality was contradictory at that time.

I believed in God, but my thinking was warped. My thoughts crossed wires and fought to overrule one another like a tangled ball of multicolored yarn. I didn't understand why I felt so defeated and depressed all the time. My inability to focus, my incapacity to sleep, and my irritability as a result showed all the signs of overthinking, and especially evidence of thinking on the wrong things. Finally hitting my breaking point, one week I was convicted of keeping track of my thoughts by writing them down in a journal. To remove distractions that led me to be mindless, I took a 3-day social media detox in addition. Throughout the day, I made a note of what I was thinking about and without judgment allowed myself the permission to write the good, bad, and the ugly. I didn't try to control the thoughts or reroute them, but I took inventory of them. By the end of my little experiment, the pages of my journal were almost eight pages of offloading years of compacted things; things I never got to say, words I really wanted to say and couldn't, pent up fears and deep inner longings. If I recall one of the confessions that came about while on my man-fast was how much I actually hated being single, how I was turning green by the couple goals around me, and ready for God to hurry up and send me 'the one'. I am certain that God adores our moments of complete openness and transparency because what we are willing to honestly confess He can now address. Before that, I didn't much consider the thought patterns I was forming or allowing to pass through my mind.

Our minds can become a garbage dump. We meditate on the wrong things; roll over the memories of shoulda, coulda, woulda; and focus on all of life's shortcomings. We delve into insecurity and inadequacy by thinking wrong thoughts, such as, "I'm not good enough." We dwell on thoughts that lead to feelings of anger, resentment, and bitterness—and those things arrest our perspectives. We meditate on other people's lives to the point that it paralyzes us and keeps us from living authentically. Then our minds get saturated with song lyrics promoting hatred, greed, and low self-worth. Add the mental calisthenics of the media's fake news, an obsession with graphic coverage of violence, and platforms of mind-numbing reality TV shows. It's a mess and completely understandable if we find ourselves not thinking correctly.

Consider that everything you receive through your ear gates and your eye gates is like a seed being sown in the garden of your mind or a root forming at the base of the tree. If a gate is a means of access or passage, what will the things that you absorb produce in your life? If what you take in, meditate on, or digest is right, you will be like a well-watered conservatory. If, however, all you have coming in is pollution, your life, countenance, and actions will surely reveal it. Where the mind goes, the whole person follows. Where are your thoughts leading you?

Society might consider it bizarre or careless if a mom was not worried and anxious about her children. Or it might seem entirely unrealistic if a person who lost her job was not doubtful and afraid. We don't believe that God can give us true peace through all of life's storms when we should. We don't see the need for being self-governing over a restless mind because we don't understand that by not doing so, we are tossed to and fro with every trend. Our mind-sets are confined; that, therefore, makes it possible for people to walk about smiling graciously in public day after day while their internal dialogue remains a mess.

Whatever you and I think is important to an omniscient God. He knows our thoughts before we even think them (Psalm 139:2).

What Are You Saying?

What have you been saying lately? What is the fruit of your thoughts? What does your internal dialogue sound like? Are you underestimating the weight of your words and the gravity that they possess?

> The tongue can bring *death or life*; those who love to talk will reap the consequences. (Proverbs 18:21 NLT, emphasis added)

The above scripture is an eye-opener because our speech reveals our thoughts as much as our actions do. I remember when I first read it, and God proposed a question to me that made me recognize my need to change the way that I was speaking about others and about myself. He asked me, "Langré, what if the things you think and say about others showed up on the skin of people like lesions or lacerations?" This rattled me a bit; my thoughts were critical of myself, but I also did not take any of my critical thoughts captive when it came to others. When I pondered this question, I had a vision of men and women walking around with daggers, spears, knives, and swords piercing their graffiti bodies. I pictured what a horror scene this would be if we were surrounded by this reality because of people's thoughts and words about each other, including our own.

When we think about the words we speak, we continuously have to ask ourselves if they are bringing life—vivacity, liveliness, energy, vigor, fire, zest, enthusiasm, spirit—or if they are contributing to death—collapse, destruction, darkness, downfall. This is why it is essential to understand why we need a tender heart and a renewed mind so that what we think and what we say can align with the Spirit of God.

Mind Transformation

And now, dear brothers and sisters, one final thing; *Fix your thoughts on what is true, and honorable, and right, and pure, and lovely, and admirable. Think about things that are excellent and worthy of praise.* (Philippians 4:8 NIV, emphasis added)

My mind used to be like an overgrown garden full of weeds. The beautiful flowers had been suffocated, and unwanted "creatures" sought to claim dominion. I imagine these creatures would look like gac fruit personified – those things are hideous to look at, although I'm sure they taste delicious. Each morning (sometimes before my feet would even touch the floor), I would find myself mentally exhausted as I tried to ward off relentless pessimism, anxiety about my never-ending to-do list, and general self-loathing. I was starting to become one of those "miserable Christians," which is a complete oxymoron. I wanted to have the joy, zeal, and peace that the Bible said I could have, but I just didn't *think* it was for me. I thought it was only for those people who had sunnier dispositions—you know, the ones who had a better start in life or who had the great career and marriage. I didn't *think* much about the condition of my mind or how my rolling over these defeating thoughts was impacting my health and general well-being.

My wandering and wondering, doubting and unbelieving, anxious and worrying, judgmental and confused mind was an issue—and it was not normal. The Bible shows us what we are to do when it comes to wrong thinking. It encourages us to "take every thought captive."

> We demolish arguments and every pretension that sets itself up against the knowledge of God, and *we take captive every thought to make it obedient to Christ.* (2 Corinthians 10:5, emphasis added)

To take a wrong thought captive means we don't suppress them; we deal with them because what we don't confront will persist. We can't have toxic thoughts and memories hanging around, making us sick, stuck, bitter, unhealthy, and angry. The reality is that people are dying fifteen to twenty years younger than the average 77 year life expectancy in the United States from preventable lifestyle diseases, according to the Centers for Disease Control. Many of these sicknesses explicitly relate to our thinking and how we manage our minds and diets. Death is not limited to dying physically, however, as people die spiritually each day and from faltering in their minds.

In the Greek, the word for "sound mind" is taken from the word *sophroneo*, which is a compound word combining *sodzo* and *phroneo*. The Greek word *sodzo* means to be saved or delivered. It suggests something that is delivered, rescued, revived, salvaged, and protected and is now safe and secure. This was God's original plan for our minds. The second part of the phrase "sound mind" comes from the Greek word *phroneo*, which carries the idea of a person's intelligence or whole frame of thinking, including his rationale, logic, and emotions. The word *phroneo* refers to every part of the human mind, including all the processes that are engaged in making the mind function and come to conclusions.

God's Word and the Holy Spirit work can save, deliver, and salvage your mind. It means that the illogical and absurd thoughts that once ruled your mind can be overcome.

Different Perspective

Our ability to pay attention to our thinking is a beautiful thing. The scientific term for our capacity to do this is called "multiple perspective advantage," or MPA, and it is the ability to "stand outside" ourselves and observe our own thinking. It is our God-given skill to look at things from a different point of view than our own. This is what so many of us need in our lives—a different perspective. This is what I needed in my life. More than asking another person for his or her opinion, however, the major key that we need is a *God-perspective*.

We may have a billion-dollar human-perspective industry that's accompanied by feel-good slogans, remarkable marketing strategies, and enticing quick tips on how to influence our environment, but we are missing the Divine Strategist who seeks to transform minds for long-lasting results. His tried-and-true method breaks strongholds of lousy-thinking habits and can cause us to be made new in the midst of our environments, families, and friends. His encouraging slogan contradicts the notion that we need to try hard, do more, or to take a special drug. No, his motto says, "Trust in the Lord with all your heart; and lean not on your own understanding. In all your ways acknowledge him, and he will direct your path" (Proverbs 3:5–6). It's not self-help; it's God-help.

With a shift to a God-perspective, we can think differently. When we think differently, we walk differently. When we walk differently, we communicate differently.

> **Do not be conformed to this world, but *be*** ***transformed by the renewing of your mind*,** **that you may prove what is that good** **and acceptable and perfect will of God.** **(Romans 12:2 NKJV, emphasis added)**

I want to challenge you to consider how your mind and brain work because it is a testament to how wonderfully and intricately God created us. While writing this chapter, I thoroughly enjoyed studying and learning more facts and scientific research on the topic. Mind renewal and right thinking start with the understanding that peace of mind and clarity of mind are our inheritance. By taking inventory of our thoughts throughout the day, we can get a snapshot of what we have been meditating on and see how our lives reflect it. As we do this, we can take the Word of God and replace whatever lie, anxious thought, and wrong perspective we've had with the truth. God's will for us was never for us to live in a state of perpetual mental confusion but to glorify him with our intellect and flourish in right thinking. Choose to serve Him today with all of your mind.

For I will take you out of the nations; I will
gather you from all the countries and bring
you back into your own land. I will sprinkle
clean water on you, and you will be clean; I
will cleanse you from all your impurities and
from all your idols. I will give you a new heart
and put a new spirit in you; I will remove
from you your heart of stone and give you
a heart of flesh. And I will put my Spirit in
you and move you to follow my decrees and
be careful to keep my laws. Then you will
live in the land I gave your ancestors; you
will be my people, and I will be your God.

EZEKIEL 36:24–28 (NIV)

Chapter 3

Identity

The crime of identity theft is when someone obtains key pieces of information to impersonate someone else. This thief robs the other person and himself or herself of being originals, as God intended. One of the popular methods used to get information is called *shoulder surfing*. The thief stands next to someone in a public venue and observes, lurking and surveillancing to gather any information they can pick up and steal from a person. Many of us have watched people walk in their originality, and instead of walking in our own, we are shoulder surfing for someone else's identity. We see something working for someone else, and so we think that if we dress like that person, or talk like him, or do what she does, we will obtain those results. We are professionals at identity theft. Imitation is not the sincerest form of flattery but the ultimate disrespect before God. We were designed to be originals—the best version of ourselves, as God intended.

> Before I formed you in the womb *I knew*
> *you* before you were born *I set you apart; I*

appointed you as a prophet to the nations.
(Jeremiah 1:5 NIV, emphasis added)

In the above verse, we see God speaking to Jeremiah, saying that he knew him Jeremiah and appointed him to do something unique with his life. In the same way that God said this to Jeremiah, he also urges us to understand that he created us. He knit us together in our mothers' wombs; he birthed us into the world on the day that we were born to accomplish something only we can do. *And therefore, he alone knows exactly who we are.* Our identity is not to be determined by or said to us by anyone else but Him.

Who Are You?

Everyone struggles with the universal question, "Who am I?" Let's consider who you were before the world told you who you should be.

A lack of understanding our identity is what drives our need to align with something that can often be detrimental. It's what births gang involvement. It causes many of us to "go with the flow," without considering that *flow* that we're going in. It potentially can evolve into dissociative identity disorder (DID), which is ultimately identity fragmentation. Misunderstood identity causes us to spend much of our lives "trying things on," instead of walking in the freedom and confidence of knowing who we are and then focusing our energies on accomplishing what we have been created to do.

In this era, there are many conversations on individuality. People are exchanging more openly about their feelings concerning aspects of themselves they are desiring to express. The dialogue on identity is a timely subject. Whether we are talking about race, gender, or sexuality, identity is the focus.

Finding your true identity will never come from this world or from another human being. If you look to another human to tell you who you are, you will always be misled because it will be based on that person's perceptions and experiences. You cannot trust the world to say who you are because society is always changing and adapting to the trends of the time. Therefore, identity comes from God alone. People who speak into your life should confirm what God has already spoken to you about you. Sometimes God will use someone to articulate who you are for the first time in your hearing. An example would be a teacher or a prophet. He can use them to bring his purpose to your awareness.

So what do we do about the current understanding of our identities? How do we view them? How have our identities been shaped for years—maybe even decades?

> Surely I was *brought forth in iniquity; I was sinful when my mother conceived me.* (Psalm 51:5, emphasis added)

What Are You Made Of?

If I were to present the current makeup of our identities as a metaphor, it would be a bedroom. The bedroom is an intimate and private place. Unlike the living room, dining room, or bathroom, not everyone should have access to this your bedroom. It is your sanctuary, your fortress of solitude. The bedroom is a place that you usually can decorate as you like to express your unique style.

In the bedroom of your soul, there are several different spaces. You and I hold many things dear in here, including our fondest memories, our values, special people, and memorable moments. When you know the purpose of a bedroom, there is peace, rest, and order. When it's clean and fresh, you are content to spend time in it. This is an enjoyable atmosphere.

A room can also get disorderly and dirty, as can our souls. We also may hold on to negative things, like grudges, anger, and hatred in our hearts. It's like walking into a cluttered bedroom. Stuff is thrown everywhere. Clothes, shoes, and bags are stuffed into every corner, along with dirty plates, pet hair, and half-empty bottles. The resident of this kind of room might consider this normal and not question the state it's in because regular cleaning has not been a priority. This room contains items that have been around for decades—clothing that doesn't fit (grudges), memorabilia from what used to be (regret), and only a dirty mirror to gaze into (distorted identity). If you've ever watched the show *Hoarders*, then you get the description I'm talking about.

You probably can vividly picture this overwhelming and out-of-control state. These individuals just keep collecting more and more *stuff*. It buries their world. It may even become a place of comfort, fulfilling a deep emotional void, and is justified by all sorts of reasons and excuses. People who collect so many different items may reach a point where they are aware there is a problem, but with their life in utter disarray, the demands of the habit, and the upkeep to maintain the large volume of accumulation, they feel helpless, lost, and confused. Let's pretend that our identities can become like this room.

You may have acquired a heavy load over the course of your life. Maybe the words people have said about you have impacted your beliefs and the way you see yourself. Perhaps someone in the fourth grade told you that you were stupid, and for the rest of your life, those words have echoed throughout your reality. Or maybe it was your cousin who said that you can't sing, and although you love to sing and often dream about it, you shy away from any opportunity to share your gift with the world because of those words. Or maybe you made a decision when you were seventeen years old that your small-town community would not let you move on. You are sensitive to the whispers and the gossip of the townsfolk. And you've decided that if people are going to label you in a certain way, you're either going to work tirelessly to prove everyone wrong or become precisely what everyone already says you are. Maybe you've seen confidence or freedom in others, and you believe that if you did as they do, you would obtain the same results. Perhaps you went through a very traumatic experience, like the loss of a parent or physical or sexual abuse, and you never got to talk about it. Things have deeply embedded themselves within your mind and have shown up in your behavior, and now you believe they are a part of your identity. The unique scenarios are unending.

On the inside, you feel the tension and the stress; wearing someone else's clothing just doesn't feel right on you. Suppressing your love and passion for something causes you to live with insecurity instead of the freedom to soar in your gift and authenticity. The level of knowledge or abandonment of your true identity, as with the condition of your mind, determines your course in life.

True identity and purpose come only from God.

Can you think of something that was said or done to you in the past that still sticks with you today? Can you see evidence of how that comment, experience, or action has rooted itself somewhere in your belief about yourself? These situations cut like a knife. They cause you to shrink inward, isolate, and distort your perception of yourself. Then, you spend so much of the rest of your life looking for your true identity and in pursuit to reclaim it. The problem is, you may not turn to God.

It is possible to become captivated by dysfunction, addicted to being in this state of limbo, and burdened by living in and with the chaos it brings, all while never questioning if this is normal. Rarely will we stop to think how life circumstances have impacted us and weighed on the persons we are today. And perhaps we've never heard anyone tell us differently than whatever has been our standard.

I can clearly see that in the past, much of my identity was wrapped up in the people I was around. My character did not come from an inner knowing and certainly not from God. I spent a lot of time "trying things on"—trying on different clothing trends, searching through my ancestry, seeking validation from relationships, looking for someone—anyone— to tell me who Langré was. I didn't know, and I could not figure it out. People often couldn't distinguish me from the people I was around. I blended in; I did not stand out. I shrunk back, and as a result, I became envious of those who walked boldly and confidently, assured of who they were.

The Good News

The hardest part of cleaning a cluttered space is the removal and renovation process. This is one of the many reasons people settle for what is good instead of cultivating what is needed to have what is best. We feel an ongoing internal war when we are not living purposefully. Our egos crave comfort, ease, and quantity, but our souls scream for quality, fulfillment, and joy.

Jesus then becomes the one who comes to clean our hearts and reveal our true identities.

That is what it can be like when we invite Jesus into our lives. What we have been upholding as correct (our understanding of life) can swiftly be shifted when he is welcomed into our lives. Our many years of trying to figure out life on our own—carrying around regret, shame, and guilt—can (and does) get lifted from our hearts the moment we accept what he did for us on the cross.

Goodbye Old Identity

> This means that anyone who belongs to Christ has *become a new person*. The old life is gone; a new life has begun! (2 Corinthians 5:17, emphasis added)

I recall watching a demolition of a derelict property. It took only a day to tear down what had stood erect for decades. The men who demolished the building had a plan in place before putting the tools in motion that day. It is so for our lives too.

Long before you even picked up this book, the Lord was

sending you little nudges through people, circumstances, or posts that you came across online. He's had a plan in place all this time for you to invite him into your heart (your room) so he can help you clean it up, set order to it, and give you the internal serenity you have been looking for externally. He desires to heal you from false-identity, to remove the mask you wear and to introduce you to your authentic self, revealed in Christ Jesus.

Walking with God and allowing his Holy Spirit to form a separation between what we should keep and what we should purge happens when we renew our minds by reading the Bible. When we study the Word, we begin to disconnect the old wiring (wrong mind-sets). Drywall gets knocked down (emotional baggage), and our plumping gets replaced (desires/will). Sometimes in this demolition process, we get stripped down until only the foundation remains.

> Therefore, since you have been raised with Christ, *strive for the things above*, where Christ is seated at the right hand of God. Set your minds on things above, not on earthly things. *For you died, and your life is now hidden with Christ in God.* When Christ, who is your life, appears, then you also will appear with Him in glory.
>
> Put to death, therefore, the components of your earthly nature: sexual immorality, impurity, lust, evil desires, and greed, which is idolatry. Because of these, the wrath of God is coming on the sons of

disobedience when you lived among them, you also used to walk in these ways. But now you must put aside all such things as these: anger, rage, malice, slander, and filthy language from your mouth.

Do not lie to one another, *since you have taken off the old self with its practices, and have put on the new self, which is being renewed in knowledge in the image of its Creator.* (Colossians 3:1–10, emphasis added)

The Restorer of Identity

If you continue walking in your current understanding of who you think you are, how much of that is based on people's impressions and society's labeling? If you keep exhausting your mind, emotions, time, and resources by continuing to hold on to everything you have experienced until now, how will you feel when you're living without the things you deeply desire, such as love, joy, freedom, and peace?

Faith is trusting and believing God for something, even when we have zero evidence that it's possible. Faith keeps us going. We all need something that keeps us believing, hoping, and petitioning to see something flourish in our lives and in the lives of others. We exercise faith every single day, whether we know it or not. Faith is a muscle that must be used if we are to be brave enough to step into unfamiliar territory.

We have a responsibility to sit with God and invite him to create in us a clean heart, heal us of distorted identity, and renew in us a steadfast spirit. We have to allow him to take some bleach and maybe even some bug spray to our stinking thinking, our habits, our appetites, and our "normal." We need to ask him to shine a light on the situations that are going on in our lives to bring clarity to what we should fight for and what we should take our hands off. It's time to break the addiction we have to living dysfunctional lives and learn to love and appreciate order, peace, and a single and whole identity.

Chapter 4

Effects of Broken Relationships

Some of us have tried to develop entire lives on a foundation of sand. It's possible that our bases were faulty from the get-go, and we have never stopped to analyze or question the conditions on which we have been attempting to build. Constructing a home on such ground can be tough, and the problems are numerous. (Google "houses built on sand," and you will get a general idea of what I mean.)

The problem of a faulty foundation does not show up immediately, but usually, you can pinpoint issues over time. The foundation of a physical home is buried, so problems can be hard to detect right away. Over time, however, the immense pressure of a building and the ground around it can cause these foundations to crack. Signs of a faulty foundation could be doors that will not open or close smoothly, or floors that feel unleveled as you walk. When this happens, a foundation repair specialist is called in. This structural engineer can inspect the property and advise on what needs to be done. His or her job is to survey the damage, assess the ground beneath, and repair the foundation.

Like these properties, we are called to revisit our foundations and have them rebuilt upon something (or someone) that is solid. When we allow Jesus Christ into our lives, he then acts like the structural engineer. The role of a structural engineer is crucial in the construction process. Unlike architects, who focus on the appearance, shape, size, and use of the buildings, structural engineers must solve technical problems. Before work can begin, they are involved in the investigation and survey of the build sites to determine the suitability of the earth. Like these engineers, Jesus is all-hands-on-deck in our lives, surveying our environment, concerned for our safety, and in charge of the necessities for the construction process. He is our on-site supervisor for this project.

> Everyone then who hears these words of mine and does them will be like *a wise man who built his house on the rock*. And the rain fell, and the floods came, and the winds blew and beat on that house, *but it did not fall, because it had been founded on the rock*. And everyone who hears these words of mine and does not do them will be like *a foolish man who built his house on the sand*. And the rain fell, and the floods came, and the winds blew and beat against that house, and it fell, and great was the fall of it. (Matthew 7:24–25, emphasis added)

I encourage every one of us (especially those of us who are not married) to take advantage of alone time. For those of you who are married, create a set time (thirty minutes to an hour, if you can spare) to get somewhere quiet and by yourself. Time spent alone provides us with the opportunity to evaluate our infrastructure. There is no way that any structure can be built without a proper and healthy foundation.

As I mentioned in chapter 1, you can be and do many things while still functioning in a fragmented soulish state. You can have a ring on your finger but always find yourself searching for an identity. You can successfully live as one of the "walking dead," unable to connect with others. In other words, you are alive physically but wholly disconnected and disengaged in your everyday life. You can function in your relationships without even acknowledging that there is a broken connection or detachment. Instead of experiencing growth in its abundance, you live with a divide.

In the Beginning

From the time we are born, we experience relationships with other human beings. For some, thinking about the history of their relations brings many joyful memories of their childhood, adolescence, and adulthood. Regretfully, though, many individuals don't have the best experiences from all the complexities that come with these associations.

Below the surface of those who seem more challenging to understand and to build a connection with can be deeper roots, going back to their foundations. People may judge the messiness, sin, promiscuity, addiction, and poverty of spirit, but

God sees his creations in need of his grace, mercy, and total restoration. It's tempting to pull away from those individuals, but as we imitate Christ, he is our example of loving the broken, the rejected, the downcast, and the misunderstood. As we allow God to dig into our own lives, we should see ourselves healing and transforming, thus, we will become patient, compassionate, and merciful toward ourselves and others. He sees our houses built on sand and offers us the opportunity to create a new foundation on solid rock.

Shaped by Unhealthy Relationships

It's rare that people intentionally set out to pursue toxic relationships. When you have been wrapped in dysfunction, however, combined with emotional and physical dependence, you may be tempted to overlook that you might be a toxic person. You may be the one who is the most harmful to your own destiny and purpose-filled life. It's a hard reality to swallow. "Unhealthy" becomes the norm. We can continuously cycle in harmful practices, and we often need divine help to see this clearly.

Perhaps your troubles trace back to a broken home. You may have experienced some form of abuse, struggled throughout life with low self-esteem, carried a weighty burden of guilt and shame, or encountered an array of things. As I write this chapter, the United States government has just implemented action that has caused separation of children from their parents at the border of Mexico and the United States. No matter the reasons behind these immigrants' flight to the US, the separation of young children from their parents causes unnecessary trauma.

Time will reveal the implications and the complications of this action.

With that said, many people from different backgrounds and circumstances have experienced cracks in their foundation. I will discuss the importance of taking responsibility for our own lives and decisions, but it would be a disservice not to examine our individual histories and upbringings; doing so can help to set us on a path to healing and wholeness.

What are some of the broken relationships in which you have found yourself? What are some of their effects? Let's take a look at the foundation.

Broken Families

I once said that the hardest part about growing up is learning that your superman is actually Clark Kent and your superheroes, too, have their unique weaknesses. Perhaps you've heard the saying, "You can pick your friends, but you can't pick your family." Adulthood is learning the truth that people have strengths and they also have kryptonite. Our guardians, as perfectly and completely as any flawed human being can, give us what is within their capacity to provide; emotionally, mentally, physically and spiritually. For some, that infilling may have been more than others. Sadly, many of us come from two or three generations of broken homes, through no fault of our own.

A broken home is considered to be a single-parent household. This could be the result of separation, death, divorce, out-of-wedlock birth, guardianship, or other factors. For the first few years of our lives, the people who comprise our homes are those who help shape and enforce our personalities, outlooks, value systems, and moral beliefs. When there is brokenness in this area, it affects us. Many of the health difficulties that affect kids from broken homes are related to mental health—the psychological side of things. The statistics for single-parent households are staggering.

In 2003, the *Lancet*, a peer-reviewed medical journal, published a study on about one million children who were followed for a decade, into their mid-twenties. The study found that children who grew up in single-parent households were twice as likely to develop psychiatric illnesses (such as severe depression) and addictions (such as alcohol dependency) later in life.

As a child who grew up in a single-parent home—due to the loss of my father at age eleven—I was able to identify with specific information I encountered during my research. From the time of my dad's passing, I struggled with my self-confidence and self-worth. I fought the need to compare myself to others. Additionally, I took on the mind-set from a young age that I needed to be responsible. Although that is a positive attribute, it was distorted because I somehow managed to believe that *everything* was my responsibility. I often felt overly anxious, got easily stressed, and was prone to depression.

My low self-worth caused me to engage in a more promiscuous lifestyle, as I often needed the validation, attention, and a false sense of love that lust brought. These things were highlighted even more in the beginning stages of revisiting my foundation and allowing God to show me my *why*. It was uncomfortable, to say the least. Reading the scriptures was like having someone shine a light on all of the dark places. It exposed them so that they could be corrected. It placed a mirror right in front of me and encouraged me to see me—all of me—from the beginning to the present day. Until I was able to see my behaviors for what they were, I remained ignorant of them, and I reasoned that they were just the way I was.

Nevertheless, let's not limit this section to *only* the effects of being raised in a one-parent household. That is far too heavy a burden to place upon solo parents who frequently go above and beyond what they can do for their children. In my research, I found that dysfunctional households, including dysfunctional two-parent families, have an equally damaging effect on children.

The effects of growing up in a home where there is constant bickering, unhappiness, belittling, and so forth are not always immediately evident. Some feelings fester and then manifest in different negative ways down the road. Growing up in a family where adults treat one another with total apathy, mere tolerance, or even contempt is felt by all residents of that home. A loveless home can be as destructive as a broken home.

Joyce Meyer, who is one of my favorite teachers, often shares her testimony of the sexual, emotional, and mental abuse she endured at the hands of her own father. In addition to her father's molestation of her, her mother became passive in confronting the problem and did not leave her husband, despite her awareness of the ongoing abuse. This birthed many deep-rooted issues that, by the grace of God and her own process, she was able to find healing for later in life. She attributes much of her transformation to diligently studying the Bible, praying, and applying its principles practically. Her ministry has continued to be a conduit of hope to many hopeless, lost, and fragmented souls. With a loving and supportive husband, a determination for healing, and God on her side, she was able to overcome.

My mother was the child of a family environment in which family members carried an air of contempt and disdain for one another. Women often do not understand the significance of the words they speak and the importance of their overall well-being while being pregnant with child. Due to marital difficulties and a challenging delivery, my mother developed a root of abandonment from the time of her birth. I believe that Satan (who is alive and well) seeks to plant a seed in people's lives as early as he can so that he can reinforce it and gain a foothold in their minds, personalities, and functionality over the years.

Consequently, further poor choices and lack of knowledge and understanding about how to cultivate my mom's vibrant and curious personality only created deeper roots of disconnect. When I think of her life and what she endured, I find it incredibly amazing that she has forgiven every wrong and decided not to allow bitterness and resentment to rule over her. Every single day, she chooses to have joy, gratitude, and love. She is the wisest and most resilient woman I know.

The effects of a broken or dysfunctional home are boundless. As you're reading this section, maybe you are looking over your foundation. If so, I want to encourage you not to point blame or feel shame but to acknowledge that there is a cause and effect for why we are the way we are and why we do the things we do. Remember that the issue isn't a people problem; it's a sin problem and all people have been infected. As long as there is sin in the world, we will be confronted with the well-meaning, but usually mark-missing, often selfish, mean-spirited, and at times out right evilness of others. Thank God for a Savior who helps us to walk victoriously, despite our past mishaps!

> I may not be where I want to be, but thank God I'm not where I used to be. I'm okay, and I'm on my way.
>
> —JOYCE MEYER

Divorce

Sometimes divorce transpires. Some marriages go the extra mile; others do not. We never imagine that divorce will occur in our lives, but when affairs are committed and safety concerns unfold, we can't always stick it out in a broken marriage. In America, there is one divorce approximately every thirty-six seconds. That's nearly 2,400 divorces per day; 16,800 divorces per week; and 876,000 divorces per year. The average length of a marriage that ends in divorce is eight years.

Forty-three percent of children growing up in America today are being raised without their fathers. Divorce may be something that most adults can live with, but when there are kids involved, things can get complicated.

If you have ever spoken to a person who has gone through a divorce, you've likely heard a mixture of pain, regret, and—at times—relief. One of the reasons divorce is so painful is that it's ultimately the severing of one flesh. In Genesis 2:24, God says that through the covenant of marriage, a man and a woman cling to one another and become one flesh (or one person). Marriage, then, is the gluing together of two persons.

Let's say you have two pieces of cardboard and you superglue them together. They are completely attached. What would happen if you attempted to pull these pieces apart? More than likely, they wouldn't tear apart very smoothly. This would be difficult to do, and it's possible that the parts wouldn't look the same as they did before being glued together. Divorce is the equivalent of tearing apart these two pieces of cardboard.

In addition to the severing of two people who have become one, there is an impact on any children involved. The research included in *The Truth about Children and Divorce* tells us that children of divorced couples can and do go on to be remarkably resilient. However, this life-changing event is *always* stressful for them. Most children do not want their parents to separate (unless the home is filled with conflict, anger, and other forms of misery). This transition can be calm or an overwhelming, chaotic time.

Divorce increases the risk that children will suffer from behavioral and psychological problems. These may include displays of anger, disobedience, and rebelliousness and depression, anxiety, and being overly responsible for caring for their parents instead of seeking care from them. Divorce can and often does impact the relationship between parent and child. Even resilient children will regularly report ongoing worries and painful memories.

I believe this is why God admonishes us through his Word not to proceed into marriage haphazardly. There are specific instructions, wisdom, and insight into how men and women are to approach marriage and safeguard it. Unfortunately, though, because people do not understand what a union represents or what their marriage is intended to accomplish, they abuse it.

Instead of exercising careful consideration, many just want to be married for the sake of it. Anyone who has been married will encourage you to use wisdom, enjoy the process, and understand what caring for another person involves.

Marriage is work, and it is a ministry. It often is meant to make us holy (more Christlike) instead of merely happy. God is the glue that will hold you and your spouse together. Without God, the many things that seek to bring about division and divorce will be much more difficult to ward off.

This is not to shame anybody who has gotten a divorce because a large number of children of divorce feel and function like kids whose parents are married. There is forgiveness, mercy, and grace for *all of us*. If you felt a heaviness as you read this, pause, and take a deep breath. We're going to make it through this book with singleness of heart, wholeness, and healing in mind.

There is life after divorce. God can, does, and will restore everything you have lost if you put him first and allow him to heal every broken ridge that may have resulted from this separation. There is also power, counseling, and wisdom made available for reconciliation and restoration of said marriages too. Singles, we can choose to become more proactive against perpetuating more generations of brokenness by allowing ourselves to submit to and engage fully in the single-season process and by permitting God's Word to be our standard in courting, selecting a spouse, and marriage.

Society should make every effort to support healthy marriages and to discourage married couples from divorcing. I believe we will be a generation that marries with purpose and produces continual generational blessings of honoring matrimony *and* monogamy.

Friendships

Friends come in all different hues. A friend is a person you know and with whom you have a bond of mutual affection, typically exclusive of sexual or family relationships. A friend is characteristically someone you can trust, an ally in times of struggle and for a cause. A friend is someone who will support you, sympathize with you, and remain loyal to you. Friendships are vitally important to our overall success and well-being.

But let's be honest—our friends have not always been our allies in times of need or our greatest cheerleaders. Over the course of our lives, the dynamics of our circles change as we evolve.

You've probably heard the saying, "It takes a friend to be a friend." In other words, to have great friendships from which you receive respect and support, you must also give respect and support. For someone to celebrate you in the capacity you wish, you will probably be presented with the opportunity to rejoice on that level with someone else. You will reap what you sow. The responsibility of maintaining any relationship means that you must learn to go beyond yourself. Unfortunately, due to selfish dispositions, friendships tend to pull from you or keep you stagnant, rather than enhance and elevate you.

People often measure success by their hard work, opportunities, and academic excellence. These are essential ingredients to turn visions into realities, but success in life comes down to the people with whom you choose to spend your time. The impact of surrounding yourself with people who can lift you higher is unmatched. Our lives are affected in many ways by the quality of those with whom we share close company. As cliché as the saying is, "Birds of a feather flock together" does indeed hold weight. We become more like the people we hang out with.

Who are the people you spend the most time with? Do they encourage you to be better or discourage you and bring you down? Are they people you can admire and grow around, or are they professionals at sitting and complaining? Do you feel motived by them or completely drained after leaving their presence?

In my early twenties, I reached a point where I was ready to change my lifestyle and make better decisions for my future. My college years, as I've already described, were characterized by lots of partying, drinking, and smoking, but over time, I no longer desired to pursue these things. Not only was I maturing, but I also saw that the consequences of keeping these things in my life outweighed the little bit of fleeting enjoyment they added to it. They were not moving me in the direction that I desired for my life. Therefore, those friendships that I developed through these common interests were put to the test to see if they would evolve beyond them. Unfortunately, they did not.

My circle shrank drastically. Those I considered "forever friends" could not grow beyond that space in which our friendships had begun. It was not an easy detachment; it was a challenge to pull away. I didn't lose love for them, but I had to acknowledge that they had an impact on my thinking and on my behavior. My interests changed, and when my desire for a different lifestyle ensued, it caused a strain on those friendships. Instead of encouraging my growth and moving forward, my friends resented it, and we came to a standstill.

This was a difficult thing to experience because our friends often can and do feel like family; separating can be taxing. Yet what else can you do when you are not going in the same direction anymore?

I realized that many of my friendships had been built on a shallow and sandy foundation. We were good as long as we had companionship in our messes, but I desired to break out of the cycles and chose something different. I had a hard time letting go. I often prayed for them. I tried to do what Jesus would do and love them "into the light," but that eventually showed me I was being self-righteous in thinking I could do what only God could do. And I realized that I did not genuinely love them if I was on a mission to change them and not accept them.

I found it a challenge to hear God tell me to pull away from these friendships—I thought it was the devil. Why would God ask me to separate from them? Wasn't I supposed to be the light and show them Jesus in my life? Didn't they need the opportunity to see how much I had changed so they would be intrigued to know God and change too?

The deception was real because the truth is, God does tell us no, and he does tell us when it's time to separate from people. Also, what pride I had to think *I* would be the one to change them. But friendships that are not anchored in God can be depleting and draining. They can be entirely consumed by gossip and drama, offer no real enhancement, and cause you to feel negative and low about yourself. Such a circle will keep you repeating your old patterns as long as you are bonded by common interests and experiences. God-centered friendships have their unique share of challenges, but they are mutually beneficial.

Friends who share a centered love for God pour into you like a fresh pitcher of water on a hot summer's day. They pray for you when you are in need. They bring out the best side of you. Although in every friendship there is the temptation to compete or to be jealous or envious, when these things arise, you are able to talk about them transparently, without condemnation, guilt, or shame. You can help each other in healing those weak areas. That's a level of openness you can rest in.

Healthy friends want to see you go forward and fulfill everything that God has called you to be and do. And—most important—when there are disagreements and conflicts, the foundation of God (the glue that holds all things together) helps you to sort them out. Without God in the midst of a relationship, when tension transpires, you're likely to be met with revenge, gossip, slander, and strife. As I said earlier, these relationships deplete you and drain you; they suck the life from you and have nothing to offer. Unhealthy friends may be happy when you do well, but only if you're not better than they are. These kinds of friendships can distract you from fulfillment and peace of mind.

A lot of unhealthy friendships that I had have dissolved. In some cases, I can humbly admit that it was because I was the toxic one. In other instances, they were. Regardless, each scenario proved its own level of difficulty, but I am grateful that, in turn, friendships marked by reciprocity, encouragement in positive things, and real accountability had room to come forward.

When you don't know or understand what it means to be a friend, you can settle for a lesser version of what true friendship means and should reflect. Remember, those with whom you surround yourself influence and impact your life. A secure social network is associated with a healthy and long life. I encourage you to trust God to bring these healthy relationships into your life—those that are authentic, grounded, and progressive. God wants us in healthy relationships with others and to thrive as we walk through life together.

> *Two people are better off than one, for they can help each other succeed.* If one person falls, the other can reach out and help. But someone who falls alone is in real trouble. Likewise, two people lying close together can keep each other warm. But how can one be warm alone? A person standing alone can be attacked and defeated, but *two can rise back-to-back and conquer.* Three are even better, for a triple-braided cord is not easily broken. (Ecclesiastes 4:9–12 NLT, emphasis added)

Healing at the Root

You are not responsible for how your beginning began, but you surely are responsible for choosing how it will be going forward. Everyone has a story. It's time to do away with behavior-modification attempts and masking our faulty foundational issues with glamorous fixed-up décor and chandeliers. It's okay to admit that we've been through some things. We've experienced hurt, and some of us may be very angry about that. It's time to begin our healing process by allowing the structural engineer into our lives so he can repair what is faulty, broken, cracked, and lost so it won't hinder us anymore. I believe that even before hiring a therapist, Jesus came to set us free from our sins and shame. His love for us covers a multitude of brokenness, and his Spirit works in our lives to put the pieces together again.

At the root of many of my issues was a need to confront my childhood and challenge my story. I needed to reverse the words that had deeply ingrained themselves in my identity by replacing them with the Word of God. I needed to separate and be separated from friendships that kept me in cycles of dysfunction. Ultimately, I had to learn the beauty in forgiving and letting go so that I could grow.

No matter what effects broken relationships have had on you, I know a great physician you can see about that. He has a way of mending the broken hearts and binding up all of the wounds. He doesn't reject you or abandon you; he walks side by side with you through every season and circumstance. His love is agape, the highest form of love there is. It involves commitment, faithfulness, and the act of the will. It's a love that is strong in character, powerful in expression, and so beautifully described in 1 Corinthians 13. It's a love that loves the unlovable and the unlovely, not because we deserve it or because we've achieved something to earn it but because it's true to his nature. God's love for us is continually seeking, always pursuing, and gracious.

This kind of love is not natural for us because of our fallen nature. It is one of the reasons why we must forgive others— because of their incapacity to produce such a love. God is the source of this love. As we learn and recognize what great love toward us is, we then can reflect that higher virtue in our relationships and toward our bitter enemies.

> But God demonstrates his own love for us in this: *While we were still sinners, Christ died for us.* (Romans 5:8 ESV, emphasis added)

Chapter 5

The Father Void

Sing to God, sing in praise of his name,
extol him who rides on the clouds;
rejoice before him—his name is the LORD.
A father to the fatherless, a
defender of widows,
is God in his holy dwelling.
God sets the lonely in families,
he leads out the prisoners with singing;
but the rebellious live in a sun-scorched land.

—PSALM 68:4–6 (NIV)

For years, I looked for protection, provision, and affection from imperfect men. I craved attention and often struggled with low self-esteem. The compliments and companionship of my male counterparts made me feel validated, and I sought it. But then, with a broken heart, a lot of bad habits related to dating patterns, and no clue who I was, I found myself tired of the search.

I remember kneeling on the floor, dampening the carpet with my waterfall of tears as I cried out to the Lord in prayer.

The year was 2016. I had just lost my stepfather to a heart attack. It was three in the morning when I got the call that he had passed away. I couldn't wrap my head around what my sister was saying on the other end of the phone; I had been sitting with him and my mom just a few hours earlier. He had been telling me everything that he thought I should do with my life—advice I greatly appreciated then and still cherish to this day.

"You should move back in with your mother and sister," he encouraged me in his thick Italian accent. *"Don't date a man who doesn't express how blessed he is to have you in his life."*

It was a warm summer day in July and we were all sitting outside of the house on white plastic patio furniture, soaking up the rays. I lamented to them my single girl woes, that I didn't think I was going to meet an eligible suitor if I remained on a small island in the middle of the Atlantic Ocean. My mom and I went back and forth about how I needed to leave Bermuda to position myself to meet someone, but his response was, *"No. Don't worry. You don't need to go far to meet someone; that someone will find you. Look—I found your mother right here."* This was the kind of reliable advice that could only come from a father's heart.

To say that going from having that conversation to finding out that he was no longer with us less than eight hours later was earth-shattering is an understatement. To say I was angry and confused is an understatement. I felt robbed. My mom patiently waited to find true love again. She, after all, had decided not to remarry while my sister and I were young so as not to complicate our upbringing more (I will always honor and respect her for that tremendous sacrifice). We had become hopeful. There were no words to comfort our grief at the time. His sons were just beginning their adult relationships with their father, and anger was justified and understandable on all fronts. For me, I was going to have a father again. I was going to gain brothers. There would be some testosterone added to our "let's talk about our feelings" girl world. Our family was going to expand. We were supposed to become a big blended family! All of our expectations of him being around came crashing down in the blink of an eye. His death gave all of us a hard reality blow, and there are many days, even now, when I believe we're still processing the reality of his absence. We each grieve differently and uniquely.

I believe that each of us has a moment in our lives when we are tempted to turn our backs on our faith and hope, but we must make a decision to not give up, no matter how harsh things get. We are sometimes deceived into thinking that a certain status or material possessions will make us exempt from the cruel realities of life. Hardship and tough times spare no one.

What kind of cruel joke is this, God? I sobbed bitterly. *You've taken every father figure I've had, and I'm supposed to relate to you as a Father? How?*

Trauma usually breaks you entirely or makes you stronger. In this case, it broke me and took me to a familiar low place on my knees again. For the second time in my life, I had lost a father and I was beyond angry about it. I thought that because I was a Bible reading, church attending, and prayer warrior I would forever be exempt from any of the troubles in life. I, apparently, had misunderstood the rawness and realness about truth about accessing grace in difficult circumstances. I found myself continuing the following expression of grief for several weeks:

"God, I no longer have any earthly father figures, so you are going to have to be who you say you are. You are going to have to protect me. You're going to have to check out these men who want to take me on a date. You're going to have to be the one to walk me down the aisle and give me away. You're going to have to be my comfort when I don't feel beautiful. You're going to have to teach me some things. You're going to have to be closer to me than ever before and heal this void I've been carrying for a father."

As I continued to cry out indignantly, it seemed that a revelation about the heart of the Father reached back towards me and was beginning to heal me and comfort me. At that moment—and I believe it was because of the transparency of my crying out before God—I felt a hand of reassurance that this request would be so. He was willing to be my Father. Up to this point, I had been very disconnected with the idea of God as a father. I couldn't relate to that. Yet, a peace of mind came upon me that could only be from the Lord in the midst of this broken place. I knew that God would indeed be and reveal himself to me in this way.

He would stand in the gap and fill the void.

How Our Father Void Affects Our Lives

I've spoken with women of various age groups on the role their fathers played in their lives. Each individual story is different. Some grew up with no dad present. Some lost a father to sickness or disease. Even those who had a father in the home have expressed a disconnect between themselves and their pops. Whichever reality it may be, when a woman carries a hole in her heart and a longing in her soul for the genuine, pure, protective, and authoritative element a father brings, there is some residue that she must take care of. Without a proper example of this in the home, we learn all kinds of warped and distorted opinions about men.

One generation of broken women potentially teaches the next how to be independent and to learn how to function in a world, not needing a man because of this absence. Brokenness because of this absence, they encourage younger women to learn how to live on guard, with one foot in and one foot out, in case a man should cheat or leave. One mother's expression of dislike, distaste, or dissatisfaction toward the child's father plants seeds of apathy in the child. Women, then, potentially grow up with hostile attitudes toward men, believing things like, "All men are dogs," "Men can't be trusted," and "There are no good men out there." They tend to act out in promiscuous behavior because of their lack of attention and love. They may practice the terrible habit of manipulating men with their emotions, words, and bodies to gain what they need. The continuation of dishonor, disrespect, and vindictiveness wears down even the strongest of men.

Therefore, the cycle continues.

How Our Father Void Affects Our View of God

Can you imagine the mind shift and rewiring it takes for God to become a Father in our reality, considering what we've discussed? When God steps into our lives, and we welcome him, we become his daughters. (Note: I didn't say we become his puppets or playthings or that we're have-it-all-together women.)

No, we become daughters.

But the problem is that we do not yet know how to be daughters with a Father present. Our knowledge of someone who loves us in a *holy, pure,* and *unconditional way* is limited because of our experiences. Our understanding of someone being protective of our emotions, hearts, and purity is contrasted by our reality of often feeling vulnerable to the rejection and disregard of these values. Our Miss Independent, hell-bent mentality leaves little willingness to understand the beauty of submission. We have become so programmed to harden our softness, reject our femininity, and even, at times, wrongly empower one another that we have lost sight of God's original purpose and the power it holds. Being a daughter of God is an honor and a privilege.

If we first acknowledge these errors in our thinking and desire to change our positions, then we might have an impact on the next generation, which not only will rock this world but also glorify and honor our Father.

The Heart of the Father

While I was in the process of writing, I felt the nudge to write down the following. I believe this is what the Lord was leading me to share concerning his heart for his girls:

> My heart is to pluck out the gold and treasure that I've placed within them. I want to set their hearts ablaze for me

and to experience the depth of my love fully. My daughters have been battered, broken, and bruised so much by the words that have been spoken over them and the situations they've had to encounter. Many of my sons have not been there to protect, care for, or provide for my daughters in the way I purposed them to do. They too suffer from ignorance and a lack of true identity.

My daughters suffer the same fate—continuing in ignorance and misplaced identity unless they repent (change their minds and their direction) and learn another way—My way.

My daughters are carrying rejection, disappointment, anger, loneliness, and abandonment so deep within their hearts. I long to reach them. I need to connect with them. I need to touch those areas that have been subjected to depression, false comfort, and self-rejection. As they are struggling with low self-esteem, I need to break the lie from their minds that they are not valuable and remind them that they are made in the likeness and image of God. I did not create half people. I desire whole, healed, and healthy people."

The heart of the Father is always reaching out to us, saying, "I desire you. I don't view you as too dirty for me to wash you clean. I don't see you as too broken, beyond my repair. I don't look at your past and cancel you out, as people do. I welcome you with open arms, willing, to love you back to life and restore you back to the soul peace of being *my* daughter."

This was life-changing for me in my walk with God because it removed the idea that he was a tyrant in heaven who was waiting to throw lightning at me and condemn me to hell if I did something wrong. This changed my understanding, and I realized that God was for me and not against me. It brought me to a love-based relationship with him and obliterated fears that I'd had. It caused me to *walk with God* (*Immanuel* means "God with us") through everyday life. I had to learn what having a perfect Father was like and how to be loved as his daughter.

> So if you sinful people know how to give good gifts to your children, how much more will *your heavenly Father* give good gifts to those who ask him. (Matthew 7:11 NLT, emphasis added)

Whatever you have experienced in this life with your earthly father or your mother, first find the room in your heart to forgive them of every wrong. Set yourself free from the mental, emotional, physical, and spiritual torment that unforgiveness breeds. Ask God to help you grasp how wide, how deep, and how vast his love is for you. Expect him to reveal it. Look for him to show it. Allow it to penetrate your heart, your reality, and your past, present, and future. Let it cover you like a warm blanket. Be engulfed in it, and don't let anyone try to convince you otherwise. Daughters, partner with your Father, who has a tendency to *restore all things* that have been lost.

> No, in all these things we are more than conquerors through him who loved us. *For I am convinced that neither death nor life, neither angels nor demons, neither the present nor the future, nor any powers, neither height nor depth, nor anything else in all creation, will be able to separate us from the love of God that is in Christ Jesus our Lord.* (Romans 8:37–39, emphasis added)

Chapter 6

Hidden Things

*O*ur secrets make us sick. Our problems, hang-ups, character traits, and habits may be obvious, but our actions were not conceived in a shallow way. They are usually nurtured by other practices. Like old school film in a camera, these things may have been developed in the "darkroom". Back in the day, special rooms were used to develop a cassette roll of photography film. In order for the images to be produced, it required the developer to turn off the lights and to be in a dark room. Any ounce of light, including even that of a cell phone, would expose the image. We may have created areas in our lives that allow us to entertain darkness and function in secrecy. What we do in the dark and in secret inevitably comes to light. As much as we would like to think we are great pretenders, we will always be fully known by God. Nothing is hidden from his sight.

> *Nothing in all creation is hidden from God's sight.* Everything is uncovered and laid bare before the eyes of him to whom we

must give account. (Hebrews 4:13 NIV,
emphasis added)

Many people have layers of hidden things that continue to
impact and affect their lives, but they feel helpless to overcome
them within their own might and effort. They spend so much
of their lives dependent on things and people to fix something,
to relieve stress, to provide pleasure that addictive dependencies
develop. We often limit the word *addiction* to a substance like
alcohol or drugs, but an addiction can be a psychological
compulsion to a wrong thought pattern. It can be extremely
tough to identify and confess, but this is why God searches for
us and lovingly points us in the direction of truth.

Don't copy the behavior and customs
of this world, but *let God transform you
into a new person by changing the way you
think*. Then you will learn to know God's
will for you, which is good and pleasing
and perfect. (Romans 12:2 NLT, emphasis
added)

When we invite God into our lives, he shows us our hiding
places—those places, people, and things we turn to for comfort
and relief. He starts to peel back those layers, one at a time.
He desires for our minds to be transformed so that we see
situations, circumstances, and people the way that he does.

In my life, I have walked with God through overcoming
several addictions—the addiction to using another person's
body for my own selfish desires; the addiction to alcohol; the

addiction to marijuana; the addiction to negative thinking. The one he's still working on is my love of coffee (you can keep me in prayer on this one).

I call them addictions because even in their infancy, I knew where continuing to walk with them would lead me. I think substance abuse is the most obvious one for which we understand the significant impact on an individual, a family, and a community. You can see it. An alcoholic did not become an alcoholic overnight; it took one glass at a time to develop dependency. Then, consider those who enabled the addict, or what about the child who now suffers from the second, third, or fourth wave of this generational addiction. God is in the bigger picture. He leads us into truth because he wants us to understand that life is not *just* about us. We were created to influence and make an impact—that's for every single one of us. The questions are, however, will it be the right influence, and how exactly will we impact it?

The Truth behind a Pornography Addiction

> Then you will *know the truth*, and the truth will set you free. (John 8:32 NIV, emphasis added)

One of the significant, life-changing revelations that I walked through with God was fully understanding what was behind my pornography addiction, how it influenced my perspective of myself and my behavior, and how it impacted others. God's standard for purity and holiness is never changing. It is concrete.

My deliverance from a roughly fifteen-year pornography

addiction came about quite somberly. Even after choosing to be abstinent and raising the standard to protect my value and my heart by reserving sex for my husband, I still struggled to let go of pornography and masturbation. My argument was, what else was I supposed to do if I wanted to abstain? I was helping myself from slipping back into the former things. Also, there was nothing in the Bible that talked about it outright—like actually saying "No pornography." I'd heard many angles to certain scriptures that argued the point, but I did what we all typically do when we don't want to do something: I twisted the verses to suit *my* desires. In my eyes, I wasn't hurting anybody. I was sure that what I did in private, behind closed doors, was hidden, secret, and not an issue. This is the deception of our own twisted hearts that I mentioned in the chapter 1.

> *Run from sexual sin!* No other sin so clearly affects the body as this one does. For sexual immorality is a sin against your own body. (I Corinthians 6:18 NLT, emphasis added)

If there's one thing I grabbed hold of it's that if you're a Christian, and you are not convicted (not condemned) about anything, question your convergence. Jesus isn't passive, wimpy, or just a prophet. No, he is the living King who comes into your life with authority and tears up everything that threatens to destroy you and ultimately lead you toward eternal separation from him. He shines a light in all the secret chambers of your heart. *It's never to destroy you but the sin nature within you!*

One day the Lord spoke to my heart that it was time to

confront another deep-seated sexual issue. What was hidden behind my four walls was not hidden from his sight. He wanted to deal with the root—why I was turning toward these things for relief and as a cure for my discomfort and loneliness instead of turning to him? God was teaching me how to turn to him for my needs instead of to these empty things. He wanted to show me how he could fulfill the scripture that promises that he will satisfy *all my requirements* in Christ. Ultimately, he wanted me to know what it meant to be chaste, modest, and pure.

Right perspective changes everything.

First, he gave me the painful truth about my addiction. He jogged my memory of the first time I went to Barcelona, Spain. I distinctly remembered walking down the streets of the city's red-light district in awe of the multitude of women lined up, soliciting their bodies to passersby. In my self-righteousness, I felt sorry for *them*. I looked upon those women with pity and sympathy as I considered what their day-to-day lives might entail. I thought how terrible it must be to service several men a day to make ends meet or to endure being pimped out, and experience intense abuse against their will.

Shortly after returning from my travels back to Bermuda, I attended a film festival that had a showing of *Nefarious: Merchant of the Souls*, a documentary that explores the global sex trade across four countries. I felt so much pain for these women as I heard their stories. Prostituted, bought, pimped, abused, traded, and sold for their bodies and for sexual pleasures. This documentary dived into the depth of the sex trade industry and revealed the lives of the sex trafficked and their traffickers.

I walked away that night questioning how they could endure that. How could God allow this to happen in our world? Why did he let it? How did it impact them mentally and emotionally? What would they have to sacrifice within themselves to fulfill their clients? Why couldn't they just leave?

In all of my questions, I shifted responsibility. I wanted to know what was God doing about this and why these people weren't protected. In the midst of my heart's breaking for answers, I received a full understanding that I was a contributor and a consumer of the problem.

What's the Cost?

According to dosomething.org, the average cost of a sex slave is ninety dollars, and there are approximately twenty to thirty million slaves in the world today. That's $27 million worth of people being sold and traded into various forms of involuntary servitude. And 80 percent of those victims are subjected to sexual exploitation (including pornography).

- Trafficking primarily involves exploitation, which comes in many forms. Victims may be forced into prostitution or forced to commit sex acts for the purpose of creating pornography.
- According to the US State Department, 600,000–800,000 people are trafficked across international borders every year, of which 80 percent are female, and half are children.
- The average age a teen enters the sex trade in the US is thirteen. Many victims are

runaway girls who were sexually abused as children.

- California is home to three of the FBI's thirteen highest child–sex-trafficking areas in the nation: Los Angeles, San Francisco, and San Diego.
- The National Human Trafficking Hotline receives more calls from Texas than any other state in the US. Fifteen percent of those calls are from the Dallas–Fort Worth area.
- Between 14,500 and 17,500 people are trafficked into the US each year.
- Human trafficking is the third largest international crime industry (behind illegal drugs and arms trafficking). It reportedly generates a profit of $32 billion every year. Of that number, $15.5 billion is made in industrialized countries.

Talk about shining a bright light on your secret stuff.

These perversions are a product of our inability to crucify our appetites. To pervert means to cause to turn away from what is right, proper, or right. It means to corrupt (someone) morally, to debase. Our society has perverted, distorted, and degenerated sex and intimacy. It has taken what was holy and pure, pimped it, put a high price on it, and figured out how to build an entire wicked empire from it. What I am about to say is harsh, but it is the truth: our lack of mind renewal, our continuance in ignorance, and our failure to exercise self-control over our appetites are contributing to the most demoralized industry in the world.

This thought process followed me into the bedroom and behind my private closed doors, and I could no longer view the people on the screen in the same way. My heart was utterly shattered that I was potentially taking delight in the disintegration and demoralization of other people. I couldn't look at it in the same way. Then, something else happened …

As I found myself bitterly weeping for their reality, I began to cry for me. And I began to weep for you. I pitied these people until one day a thought came to my mind: *What if I'm no different than her?* What if what she was forced against her will to do what I willingly did? What if I was declaring her position as prostitution but hypocritically calling mine sexual liberty? Were we not the same? Does uncommitted sexual involvement with men under the title of "boyfriend" make you or me any better than women who are forced into having sex with multiple people?

I saw my deception, and the light came and exposed what the darkness had deceived me into believing was perfectly okay. God's desire for us to be pure and holy in the area of sex is not only to protect us from the many variables that become consequences in our own lives but also to protect our world. This is why he so deeply reiterates that the only place that sex should be had is within marriage, and we are to flee even the hint of it outside of that boundary.

She and he, you and I—all are deserving of true love, acceptance, and freedom from every yoke of bondage and form of captivity. This is what Christ came and died for. Look at the bigger picture and consider these souls, consider their chains—the mental, the emotional, the spiritual, and the physical. That is a high price for our entertainment purposes. God was able to remove the scales from my eyes and bring me to see the darkness that I was habitually setting my eyes upon. In the process of talking to me about others' worth, he reminded me of mine. I was not created as an object for momentary pleasure, nor were you. This was only one example of how radically we can walk in deception and continue in a path that influences and impacts our world negatively.

But God.

He draws near to us to shine a light on our ignorance and gives us a compassionate heart for one another. We become our brother's and sister's keeper. The greatest commandment that was given to us by Jesus Christ was this:

> Jesus replied, "This is the most important: 'Hear O Israel, the Lord our God is One Lord, and you shall *love the Lord your God with all your heart* and with all your soul and with all your mind and with all your strength.' The second is this: '*Love your neighbor as yourself.*' No other commandment is greater than these." (Mark 12:29–31, emphasis added)

In Christ Jesus, we have permission to step out of the depths of darkness and into the light to be transformed by renewing our minds. Layer by layer, as God chisels at our hearts, cleaning them, and purifying them, we regain our sensitivity to him and to one another. We can lay down our destructive addictions, bad habits, and darkened conscience and become the change we wish to see.

Whatever your addiction may be, I encourage you to bring it into the light by asking God to reveal it and give you the truth about it. By your taking the time to heal, you can expose and cancel generational cycles, become a solution, and defeat the enemy that had you duped and deceived.

If you have been struggling with a pornography addiction, I recommend confessing to a trusted friend for accountability and taking the necessary steps to remove temptation from your life. There is an excellent online service, www.covenanteyes.com, that offers internet support. Because porn thrives in the shame and secrets, they offer internet accountability service that is designed to help you overcome porn by monitoring your online activity and sending a report to a trusted friend who holds you accountable for your browsing choices. This service also has many testimonials of how it has helped to rebuild trust, security, and communication for marriages by helping individuals to bypass the temptation on the internet.

Remember, whatever you starve will eventually die. God's thoughts and understanding is higher than our own, so trust him and obey when he places his hand on an area and tells you "no more."

Chapter 7

Sex, Desire, and Abstinence

Let your *fountain* be blessed, and rejoice in
the *wife* of your youth, a lovely deer, a graceful
doe. Let her breasts fill you at all times with
delight; *be intoxicated always* in her love.
—PROVERBS 5:18–19 (EMPHASIS ADDED)

"S-e-x is good." Say it with me: "Sex is beautiful. Sex is
wonderful. Sex is biblical. Sex is not dirty. We can talk
about sex. We can have this conversation. We're going to make
it through this chapter. We're going to be okay."

Unbeknownst to many, the Bible talks at great length
about two of the taboo subjects in our society: money and
sex. Money is one of the most referenced topics in the Bible.
We are given a wealth of wisdom and warnings on how to be
excellent managers of it. And sex, in all of its forms, is scattered
among the pages and woven like a tapestry of expression into
many of the most well-known stories. In every version of the
holy scriptures that I've read, sex is spoken about openly and

transparently. God, after all, is the inventor of sex. This is a topic that is near to his heart and okay for us to discuss.

Even in our shameless and overexposed society, however, we tiptoe around this conversation. We argue that it's nobody's business and not our responsibility to get a right perspective on the subject. We are, therefore, left to the world's ever-changing definition and experimentation of it. We are aware of this issue with lust because our phones, computers, radios, and TV screens are saturated with it.

Yet, for whatever reason, we do not talk about it.

There is no shortage of sex being marketed to us today. Our musical selections glorify everything but sex within marriage and abstinence. The borderline pornographic images root themselves within our subconscious and cause us to act them out in our own behaviors and thought patterns. We are becoming desensitized to the things we see, as the boundary lines are pushed farther and farther back. We often don't even bat an eye anymore. Our hearts are becoming callused as images are endlessly fed into body dysmorphia, silly comparisons, subconscious jealousy, petty competing, and a whole lot of judging.

Men are bombarded with every marketing strategy to whet their appetites and entice them with the women who Proverbs 5:3 describes as dripping like honey, with speech smoother than oil, but in the end, they are as bitter as wormwood. Wormwood is the state or source of bitterness or grief.

Sex is Beautiful

Sex is so beautiful and so powerful that it could only be safely set aside for a covenant relationship. The problem we face today is that we have taken something precious and sacred to the heart of God and between two people and diluted it into something meaningless and disposable. We should wait for marriage because we do not need to settle and compromise. We don't have to believe the devil's lies that there are no good men or good women out there, but we can exercise patience and allow God to bring our mates in his perfect timing. Courting a person and allowing things to develop gradually to see if the person presented before us is a quality candidate is far better than giving in to temptation because we lack the self-control to deny our selfish appetites. Sex was not intended to be something to satisfy ourselves; it was intended by God originally to glorify him as an act of worship and unification of a husband and a wife.

Quite frankly, I am tired of seeing women ruin their lives by giving pieces of their time, attention, hearts, and care to temporary relationships, especially when I hear of their desire for real commitment. I am burdened by the stories of men who also suffer in silence and disconnect because they never learned their true value beyond their performance in a bedroom. I am deeply saddened when I hear that abortions are considered because women feel they have no options or are afraid because the fathers won't be in the picture. I cried while watching an intervention with a man who had thirty-eight children with seventeen different women and with another who had four children by two women. It frustrates me that we forget about STDs, HIV, and AIDs and so recklessly invite strangers into our most sacred places. This breaks my heart because it's a reality that I see happening far too often. By continuing this way and not acknowledging that something is broken, we perpetuate the breakdown. We cut down ourselves, the family unit, our communities, and another generation with detachment and abandonment issues.

But here's the thing …

I do not shame anyone because God did not shame me. All of us continue in some form of ignorance until we get the truth and understanding of why God desires certain things and encourages us to walk in his will. It is for our protection.

> *Flee from sexual immorality.* Every other sin a man can commit is outside his body, but *he who sins sexually sins against his own body.* Do you not know that *your body is a temple of the Holy Spirit* who is in you, whom you have received from God? You are not your own; you were bought at a price. *Therefore glorify God with your body.* (I Corinthians 6:18–20 NIV, emphasis added)

Process of Deliverance

My story of overcoming sexual immorality is not a glamorous one. I do not reflect the cookie-cutter, pristine, "came to Jesus and everything got easier" testimony. No, my process was exactly that—a process. Have you ever heard the scripture, "the righteous falls seven times and rises again, but the wicked stumble in times of calamity" (Proverbs 24:16)? That would best suit my story; falling down seven times and getting back up again and again.

My introduction to sex as a young adult was like a rabbit hole for me. It wasn't that one day I had my innocence and then the next I was robbed of it; instead, each situation began to chip away at my integrity and seduce me into greater curiosity.

I was exposed to pornographic material for the first time when I was ten years old. A school friend of mine had the higher-number channels on her cable box. One evening, while playing in the basement of her house, she turned to one of those channels. We spent several minutes trying to make out the graphic images of two adult bodies doing something foreign to our innocent minds through the static and scrambled station. From that point on, it seemed as though sexual curiosity would set its mark to entice me at every turn.

Throughout high school, I prided myself on being a virgin, although my mind had utterly lost its thirst for purity. I wore it like a badge of honor as I blossomed into my own and started getting more attention—a likable girl who the guys couldn't reach. Yet I had already begun to develop an addiction to pornographic material. I had discovered masturbation. I had learned that my body could be a powerful tool to tease, and I continuously went a little farther than the last time. My outlook was so steeped in self-righteousness, though, that I somehow thought I was better than the girls who had had sex because I didn't go "all the way."

Over the years, I found myself in emotionally abusive relationships that were based on nothing concrete, only selfishness and confusion. In my heart of hearts, I hated feeling like the girl who was being used and treated "less than." I didn't enjoy the casual relationship of it all. I genuinely desired connectivity. I wanted someone to choose me, but all

I knew was how to use my sexuality as a tool—my first line of seduction—so I'd eventually snag a heart. I didn't know who I was, so I took on the identity of the seductress I saw in those pornographic videos. I took on the characteristics of the person I was with. I silenced the voice that told me I was worth more than being *this* girl.

My moral compass seemed to hinge on what was susceptible at the time. But in 2011, when Jesus finally got my attention, that was one of the first things he made known, loud and clear. And by that time—I'll be honest—I was so tired of feeling like a rental car. You know, a guy picks you up, takes you out, thrills you for a little while, and then goes "ghost," leaving you to ponder what happened just as feelings were beginning to evolve. Rented. Used. Returned. In that order. Truthfully, I knew nothing about sex—not real sex, that holy, sacrificial, God-designed act of worship intended to unify a husband and a wife fused by a covenant. That sex.

The information I received about abstinence was a brief five-minute lecture in between the juicier details in health class. Those who would model even a glimmer of self-denial were labeled as boring, prudish, or stuck-up. I didn't fully know what sex was, only that I shouldn't do it with someone I didn't love, and I should understand that the consequences could be long lasting. However, it was glorified on every platform. Therefore, I curiously sought to find out about it for myself.

Over time, I could see that I was taking something beautiful and turning it into a cheap thrill. It was becoming something ugly, selfish, and damaging to my femininity. I had the mentality to "act like a lady, and think like a man"; I was out to run around just as good as the boys. But now I desired to start valuing my body as the home of God's Holy Spirit. For me to become the home for the Spirit of God to dwell in, I had to allow Jesus to knock on the door of my heart and set some order to it.

As I lay across my bed, writing in my journal, I knew I needed to address this sickening feeling I had in my core. I was tired of walking about lost, guilt-ridden, and shame-stricken. Had I known God's beautiful desire for us to keep sex for the protection, covering, and sanctity of marriage, I wouldn't have had to write this painful chapter, tearfully.

I cried out, "God, I am concerned about me. I'm not in a good place right now because of sexual sin. It's destroying me spiritually, and my soul is in turmoil over the desires and pleasure of my weak flesh. It's not you; it's me. You're holy and just and sovereign. I'm a mess and even more if left to my own devices without your Holy Spirit. I'm habitually doing something that is leading me nowhere good. I'm scared to be here, to get stuck here. I'm afraid because I revere you, but my flesh feels so weak lately. My finances, my food choices, and my sexual appetite—all of these areas are out of control. But God, if you're listening to me, I still believe that as I'm confiding in you and not running from you through this, somehow you can circumcise my heart again to live for you. I don't want to stop here. I don't want to settle for temporary."

I confessed that sex outside of a marriage covenant was not what I wholeheartedly wanted or even enjoyed. It only left me feeling used, broken, unsure, and insecure. If I continued on that path, I would not have the outcome of wholeness that I pursued, but I would have continual soul fragmentation.

Controlling your sexual appetite may not be easy, depending

on your "hunger level," but it is truly beneficial for those who are willing to set boundaries, cut some people loose, and put much-required accountability in place. This is not for the lazy; it's for the diligent. It is for the men and women who can find strength through the brokenness, the hurt, and the discomfort and say, "I want God's best for my life, and I'm not settling for less." It's for the men and women who will say, "I will not prostitute my body as though I have no value."

This is for those who love a challenge, desire to master themselves, and are ready to be the champions God says they are. Saying no to sex without marriage commitment restored my value, worth, and dignity. I felt empowered because I was in the protection of God's will. There was peace in knowing that. Taking sex off the table meant that I had to learn how to view men rightly, make clean conversation, and allow the opportunity to get know one another as friends first.

Guarding my heart and upholding a standard for sexual purity taught me valuable lessons in contentment. That contentment taught me self-control; self-control taught me the beauty of faithfulness. As I became more faithful to God and to my heart, I became more patient, which turned into peace of mind, which gave me more joy, and joy provided me with the ability to love my God, myself, and others on a different level.

If you have found yourself struggling with these same things, you must know that God's original purpose for sex, his boundary for it within marriage, and his standard in this area is not going to change. He makes us uncomfortable when we are outside of his will, and our way will never satisfy. This one area is a major key in the process of restoration of your worth and confidence. Not only will you regain the power over your flesh, but you will honor God's will and desire for you to be protected within sexual purity. He will acknowledge that, keep you, and sustain you if you put your trust in him.

Your surface problems are not who you are, but they expose something that needs truth to penetrate the core and show you whose you are. You are valuable and precious to the One who created you in his likeness and image, not to be a prostitute to the world or a slave to your appetites. God does not turn away from you; it draws him in closer as you open up your entire life to him and desire true transformation. He restores your broken view of self and replaces it with the truth that he made you beautifully and wonderfully. No matter in what regard you are selling yourself short, God can raise the standards in your life and give you new desires. Sex is good. Sex is beautiful. Sex is for a marriage commitment only.

Chapter 8
The Better-Half Myth

*W*hen we were attending school and learning fractions, each of us was taught that two halves make a whole. The teacher may have demonstrated this by taking one object, such as an apple, and splitting it down the middle. Only by rejoining the two halves could we once again have a whole and complete apple.

This concept did not depart from our way of thinking. You may hear a person refer to his or her spouse as "my better half" or "my other half." This term wasn't originally reserved for one's spouse, as it is now; it could also be used to refer to a dear friend. It was used that way by the Roman poet Horace and later by Statius. The allusion then was to a friend so dear that he or she was more than half of a person's being. That meaning persists, although these days if the term is used seriously, rather than sarcastically, it is generally considered to mean "the superior half of a married couple."

The better-half concept is this: I am not complete; this other person holds a part of me. Have we been using language that implies that we are not whole people, and we expect person to complete us?

Our words have power, and so do the wrong perceptions. They can shape and mold our reality around us. We very loosely say things and repeat phrases without giving them a second thought. Let's look at this idea that another person is what contributes to completion—this is a myth that we need to address and debunk. My first question is, "Where is the other half of you?"

When we are fragmented in our souls, we tend to look for others who have what we lack or who share in our suffering. Like a magnet, we are drawn to a particular type of individual, with the expectation that he or she can fill in the missing part of us. When we have voids and fragmented areas in our souls, we often attract people who have similar missing pieces. The saying "like attracts like" applies here.

The question we need to ask ourselves is, "Are we assets or liabilities to those around us?" It is a good starting point to gauge if you like what you are attracting and what you are projecting. We need other people because we all have a need for community, a village, and togetherness. We are designed for it and for one that specifically works in love and harmony. However, without allowing for healing and a right perspective of relationships, we find ourselves in codependent scenarios.

All names and scenarios in my examples are fictitious, but I hope these stories help us see how we too can find ourselves in unequally yoked relationships.

Two Broken Halves

Brenda and Jackson met at a mutual friend's wedding. They started to date and found that they were complete opposites, something that greatly intrigued them both. They pursued a relationship that continued to evolve. Around the three-month mark, Brenda noticed that Jackson had a severe drinking problem. His social drinking was beyond the casual one to three beers a week. He often smelled like alcohol, but that didn't stop Brenda from continuing the relationship.

Brenda suffered greatly from the need to be needed. She had a "savior complex"; she felt the need to save other people. As a person with this frame of thinking, she had a strong tendency to seek people who desperately needed help and assistance, often sacrificing her own needs for them. This was a pattern that had developed in past relationships. She kept finding men who had deep-rooted issues, determining that it would be by her love, devotion, and sacrifice that they would be healed.

Jackson's issue stemmed from brokenness in his soul and a voided that had formed when his father left his mother. He used alcohol to numb the pain and forget his problems, but the escape had taken hold of him more than he'd planned.

Brenda was the oldest of all the children of her single mother. Growing up in a single-parent household developed her thinking that it was her duty to fix everything and everybody.

Brenda and Jackson remained in the nurse-and-patient-like relationship for almost eight years before Brenda had enough, and Jackson checked himself into rehab. For eight years, these two continued the ongoing cycle of trying to complete one another. Brenda needed Jackson's sickness to make herself feel valued and affirmed. Jackson needed Brenda to feel justification and a false sense of humility. He needed someone he could blame and play the victim card with. That is, he emotionally abused Brenda by making her think she was better than him and the cause of all his problems. This relationship was destructive and codependent. It was seemingly impossible to let go.

One Half and One Whole

Sandra and Michael met each other through a dating app. They exchanged numbers and began to get to know one another over the phone. Asking all of the questions and giving the perfect answers, they realized it was time to arrange a meeting in person.

Michael was everything that Sandra was looking for. She was attractive, witty, and educated and had a sense of humor. He felt he'd hit the jackpot with her. Michael was at a point in his life where he was ready to settle down and get married. He was successful in his career and in a secure place financially, with enough saved to purchase a house. His only hang-up was that he had no one to share this next chapter of his life with.

Michael knew who he was and where he was going. His pursuit of Sandra was genuine and intentional. As he began to continue dating her, however, he began to learn more about her.

Every time they got together, she was gossiping about girls at her church. She dominated the conversation, and Michael could never get a word in without her snapping at him. It was clear that she had experienced things in her past, and what he was seeing was some of the residue and effects from what had happened to her.

As time went on, although he was serious about marriage and was hoping for the best, Michael had to break things off with Sandra. He got tired of being dumped on and had to pray for her and let her go. He found that the negativity and contentiousness were too much. Her know-it-all attitude and "I don't need a man" behavior had merely turned him off. She became consumed by how much money he made and was more focused on material possessions. He couldn't afford to carry this baggage into the season he was entering.

As for Sandra, she needed more time to allow God to pluck out her wrong motives and character flaws before she married. If she had married Michael in her current state, she would have undoubtedly become more of a burden than a blessing to him.

Completion Myth

These are just two examples of how we perpetuate such confusion in male/female relationships, but this can be applied to friendships too.

> My son, if sinners entice you, do not yield to them.

> If they say, "Come along, let us lie in wait for blood, let us ambush the innocent without cause, let us swallow them alive like Sheol, and whole like those descending into the Pit.

We will find all manner of precious goods;
we will fill our houses with spoil.

Throw in your lot with us, let us all have
one purse"—*my son, do not walk the road
with them or set foot upon their path.*

For their feet run to evil, and they are
swift to shed blood.

How futile to spread the net where any
bird can see it.

*But they lie in wait for their own blood; they
ambush their own lives.*

Such is the fate of all who are greedy,
whose unjust gain takes the lives of its
possessors. (Proverbs 1:10–19, emphasis
added)

When you are looking to another flawed human being to be your everything (when you are not that yourself), depletion is inevitable. The wrong company can be detrimental to your life. In Proverbs 1:10-19 above, it's a warning of when you surround yourself and align with the wrong company. Likewise, with a romantic relationship, when you carry your emotional baggage, poor attitudes, wrong mind-set, and unrealistic expectations into another relationship and hope for someone else to make you happy, problems will arise. It's downright draining.

God intended for us to be two whole people who come together. When both persons are mutually filled, they are able to make more deposits into than withdrawals from one another's lives. God wants our foundation, identity, and security solid as a rock in him. He wants to become our anchor when storms come and our refuge when the fire kindles ... before anyone else. When God is not our go-to for healing, filling, and comfort, we make mini gods out of others through our unhealthy dependencies.

You may wonder what qualifies me to write about these different scenarios. Well, if I'm honest, I have my own share of experiences of looking to someone else to be what only God can be. In my past relationships, I have had very high expectations of my boyfriends. Often the burden I placed on them of having to do everything and to be my everything caused me much heartache and disappointment. I entered into relationships a very broken woman, unintentionally looking for saving. It took time, being single, and getting personal ministry to begin to unpack those deeper motives.

It wasn't easy, but I had to look at myself soberly. I had to admit that what I was doing was not working. I was carrying around this warped mentality of what I thought relationships should be, and there was undoubtedly residue in my heart from each failed attempt. I was picking the same kind of men. I carried the same insecurity into each relationship. I exalted my boyfriends' feelings before my own because I had no knowledge of my own worth and value. I was self-rejecting, and I carried myself into every single relationship. I was the common denominator.

Once my eyes were opened, I could see clearly that, despite

my tough-girl attitude and nonchalant mentality, these things *did* have an effect on me and the choices I was making. They also impacted the person or friend with whom I was in a relationship. As I saw me for me, with all that I was and where it was safe and appropriate, I even took steps to contact an old boyfriend and ask for forgiveness for the way I'd treated him and for my behavior. I was met with a deep conviction that we should not leave a trail of broken hearts and a future road being paved by bitterness and unforgiveness. I could see that how I engaged my relationships in the past did not reflect the spirit of God or his love.

I stopped directing the blame at every man and every person who came into my life. I had to confess that I didn't have a clue what I was doing in my relationships, and I handled them poorly. My ego then had to be silenced, and I had to express that perhaps I'd had it wrong all along. Maybe there was another way.

Yes, being single and committed to God and me was hard throughout many points. Loneliness was a factor and a battle. There is no itch like the lonely night itch that tempts you to send that text message to a familiar number you've been working hard to forget. I had to be a bit extreme in the early days by blocking numbers, deleting any doors for access, and by cutting off that sad R&B music that always seemed to set me up. I faced nights of self-pitying and self-wallowing pretending that it was going to be some kind of benefit. I eventually came to the understanding that I'm never truly alone, and the feeling of isolation is an indicator that I should reach out to my friends and family, not to hit up an ex.

I had to overcome the jealousy and coveting of others by

learning how to celebrate—*really* celebrate—their blessings, no matter if it often felt like they were getting the very thing I wanted. Whether it was an engagement, wedding, squad-goal trips, promotion, or baby announcement, I had to silence the green-eyed monster by allowing myself to sow the level of joy and celebration that I hoped to one day reap when it was my time.

I had to wrestle through the self-esteem highs and lows. When you don't have a man telling you, "You are fine," or "You look sexy," or putting heart-eyes under your picture and saying, "That's mine," you have to dig deeper to find that reassurance within yourself. When you're on a mission to get your mind and life right, you cannot put yourself out there, half naked, on social media or answering the catcalls, falling into being an internet thirst trap. You will most definitely have to guard your heart against the propositions of little introductions sent by the devil that appeal to your flesh but are undoubtedly intended to wreck your entire life and set you back.

I knew then and there that I had to pause on dating and relationships for a season. I had to be responsible for myself and stop making excuses for my poor decisions. I was able to hold a mirror to myself. Being single until I was healed enough to date again and mature enough to handle the responsibility of another person's heart was the *best thing* I could have done in this entire journey. I needed it.

Why Is This Important?

There is one who created you, the complete essence and meaning of love, and all relationships from the very beginning; that is where the solution to our interdependent relationships lie. Before anyone, there was God. In the beginning, He created everything (see Genesis 1). The reason you want to develop a relationship with God, clean up the room of your heart, and master who you are is that then you will be able to choose better relationships. If you're going to overcome anything in your life, you must first confront what's inside.

We sometimes think that another person will alleviate our internal and external dilemmas. As we've talked about in recent chapters, there is a ton of evidence that proves that is a *lie*. The truth is this: you need time to cultivate yourself as a single-whole person before joining up with another person. All of who you are, all of what you do, and all that you bring doesn't change once you get into a relationship. Actually, it becomes magnified. You can marry anybody, but another physical body in your life with his or her own thoughts, moods, and attitudes will not make a difference if you aren't secure with yourself first. It may only magnify what and who you really are. So, consider if you like the idea of having your own thoughts, moods, and attitudes amplified.

At a point in my single season, I decided that I needed to make a commitment. I was already committed to God and committed to waiting for God to send my mate, but who I had not fully committed to was myself. Thus, I bought myself a ring. I started to grasp that a ring did not determine a person's value in life. I decided I was not going to continue to idolize a ring by coveting all of the engagements and marriages around me, nor by being impatient and discontent. I walked about in the city on a sunny Bermuda afternoon to a local accessory shop. I perused the array of fabulous earrings, necklaces, and clutch purses until my eyes fell upon the thing I was looking for. It was my ring! My ring had a Roman numeral clock around the cubic zirconium diamond and was pyrite gold. Fortunately, it never turned my finger green so I could wear it every day. I was drawn to it because when I looked at it it reminded me that my prayers would be answered in the right and perfect timing. Buying myself a ring and practicing this commitment made me more mindful. I started to practice guarding my tongue against murmuring, nitpicking, and complaining. Having it was significate in helping me overcome the jealousy and envious feelings I was struggling with. Loneliness was out matched by faith and patience. I practiced cooking more for myself. I focused on self-care. Shoot, I shaved my legs and resisted the urges to buy a cat! And I became more intentional about establishing quality friendship relationships with people who would be advocates and supporters for my future marriage.

In the midst of opportunities to go off course and settle because of fear, I knew I wanted to practice commitment and faithfulness to God before meeting my spouse. I needed to exercise my faith by walking in what I didn't see quite yet. As I discerned that my time was drawing closer to meet my spouse, I started being convicted that it was vital for me to learn to carry myself as a wife beforehand. I needed to eject some of the distorted illusions in my thinking that marriage would complete me. With or without a ring on my finger, I always would have the responsibility of managing my own well-being and soul healing.

When we submit to God in this way and allow ourselves to access contentment, He comes through in the most amazing ways. When my husband proposed to me, he opened up a little red box with a diamond ring that had the exact same shape and design as the ring I bought myself (only it definitely wasn't costume jewelry). My husband who never saw my roman numeral ring because it randomly broke a year before I met him, causing me to no longer be able to wear it, ended up putting on my finger a commitment, a much awaited promise, and God's perfectly timed design. He heard every prayer.

End of the Day

No one on the face of this earth will be able to complete you. Requesting that of another person is unfair. It is far too daunting and weighty a task and too much responsibility. There is only one individual qualified to be your Savior, *just one* who can handle your casting all of your cares, fears, and anxieties on him.

Singles, we really need to acknowledge that if we are miserable in our current state, a relationship isn't going to fix that. If you are discontented single, you will be discontented married. If you cannot stand your own company, how can you expect someone else to? The feeling of being lonely does not depart when you are in a relationship. You can still be lonely, even with a pair of biceps in your bed. And if you make a relationship so important while you're single, what are you going to do when you get that relationship? You will need another thing to make you happy because you'll have received what you wanted so badly and found that it did not satisfy. This is why I love what it says in 1 Timothy 6:6: "Godliness with contentment is great gain" (NIV).

I came to accept that whoever came into my life would

only be able to complement all that I already was, and I shifted my focus toward becoming a whole individual. My happiness, contentment, and experience weren't going to be put on hold for another person's presence or absence. I made up my mind to intentionally pursue a *full* and enjoyable life while single; God willing, it will continue to spill over throughout my future marriage.

You have searched me, Lord, and you know me.
You know when I sit and when I rise;
you perceive my thoughts from afar.
You discern my going out and my lying
down; you are familiar with all my ways.
Before a word is on my tongue you,
Lord, know it completely.
You hem me in behind and before,
and you lay your hand upon me.
Such knowledge is too wonderful for
me, too lofty for me to attain.

—PSALM 139:1–6 (NIV)

Chapter 9

The Pursuit of Intimacy

I speak from a place of going through. I am not above any situation or circumstance, but I have been given the opportunity to start over, change my perspective, and break that which had a stronghold in my life.

In our present society, mixed with so much contention and pressure to follow the masses, you need to know there is a different standard to live by. As a faith-walker, you need to know there is nothing wrong with talking about honoring what you believe and what you stand for and to be proud of it—unequivocally unashamed.

The world around us feeds us sex when our souls crave intimacy. Being intimate means *into-me-see*. It's a beautiful arrangement of our hearts blending with another's so we can see into who they really are, and they can see into us. The word *intimate* is defined as "being characterized by close personal acquaintance or familiarity; relating to or indicative of one's deepest nature; very personal; innermost."

God created us to desire connection and close union.

This is not to be confused with sex. Sex can be an intimate

expression of love for another person, but it is not the substance, sustainer, or proof of love. Marriages cannot be kept together by sex, nor can sex be the sole cause for breaking a marriage— of course, a breakdown in communication or interest can contribute to the lack of sex and eventually lead to that. Sex does not guarantee alleviation from loneliness. Our entertainment industry has done a terrible job and lied to us with ample imagery of two people finding love and connection as a by-product of their sexual involvement. It may work on TV, but it's not reality for most people.

Has anyone taken the time to really look at you—to make you feel like he or she has peered into your soul and seen you in there? When Jesus said, "And the two shall become one" (Mark 10:8 NKJV), he actually meant that two people will become one through real intimacy, as opposed to the physical unification applied to his passage. I believe he knew that it was possible for people to merge their bodies and lie down next to one another every night, yet never share their hearts with one another. He knew, and I think we're coming to realize, that sexual stimulation and physical interaction with another person are not enough to cure loneliness or to tend to the personal needs within the gardens of our hearts.

Real intimacy doesn't make you feel overlooked. It makes you feel fully known. It doesn't make you feel ignored. It gives you an assurance that you are wholly accepted, just the way you are.

As I discovered through my own testimony, no matter how hard I tried, if emotional and spiritual intimacy did not exist before sex, it most certainly wouldn't afterward. Before I welcomed another person into my space and sought to build this kind of closeness, I needed to connect with my own heart intimately. I needed to find out who I was and what my fears, dreams, hopes, and desires were. I needed to ask the Lord to recall my own heart.

The thing is, this level of soul-refreshing, heart-healing, and mind-transforming intimacy begins with Jesus. You have to first reach the revelation for yourself that he died for you—the good, the bad, and the ugly. He saw you in your totality and at the innermost core of your being, and through his actions on the cross, he said, "I love her" or "I love him." Because God made us, he intimately knows us better than anyone can. Contrary to popular belief, he can make us feel fully understood and accepted in a way that no one on earth is able to do.

The challenges we face today have us screaming for closeness and connection beyond the allure of sex. We have to come up higher and acknowledge that what we are being marketed and sold is not what satisfies our souls. God is calling us back to a place of true intimacy, being fully known and accepted. He's calling us to him, so he can recall the pieces of our emotions, hearts, bodies, and identities and begin to heal genuinely. I encourage you to pursue and experience the beauty of intimacy with God.

For you created my inmost being; you knit me together in my mother's womb. I praise you because I am fearfully and wonderfully made; your works are wonderful, I know that full well. My frame was not hidden from you when I was made in the secret place when I was woven together in the depths of the earth. Your eyes saw my unformed body; all the days ordained for me were written in your book before one of them came to be. How precious to me are your thoughts, God! How vast is the sum of them! Were I to count them, they would outnumber the grains of sand—when I awake, I am still with you.

—PSALM 139:13–18 (NIV)

Chapter 10

Wholeness

I began this process of walking with God seven years ago. When I started, I was an entirely different woman than I am today. If I could liken myself to anything, it would be an onion. Interestingly enough this is what the people of Bermuda are referred as; Bermuda Onions. Like an onion, we all have many layers. We often do not see these layers by outward appearance alone, but when we allow a sharp object to cut through our tough exterior, we can see what lies underneath. When we chop onions, it can cause us to cry—a lot. A burning sensation and a distinct odor arise. However, once the layers are peeled back and then diced up and thrown over a hot fire, they give off a pleasant aroma that fills a home and enhances any dish.

I like to think this is precisely how it is with our journey of becoming single and moving toward wholeness and healing. We are challenged to make the confession that we have layers (and many of them). Then, by allowing the heart of God and the Word of God to pierce through each layer, we start to see and become who we were always meant to be. He restores our true, authentic identity.

We face the effects of our broken relationships, and we no longer play victims, shift blame, or minimize our brokenness. God reveals how faulty it is to put too much confidence in fragile human beings, yet he brings about surety and confidence in knowing who our true Source, provider, and strength is. For the first time, we get to experience what it's like to have the mask off—the power of transparency and being fully known.

Your mind regarding intimacy will be blown entirely. God will reveal to you things you've never known. He will help you to see how shallow your appetite has been. It may feel like a challenge, a stretch, and a pull to come up higher in every area of your life. You will make mistakes and find yourself in tearful repentance, turning away from the things that seem to keep you chained and bound and crying out to a merciful, loving, and forgiving Father. The weeping and discomfort last only a little while (or seven years, in my case), but the joy always follows. Don't lose hope.

You will see God in his true nature—not a mean tyrant who aims to give you a bunch of rules and who robs you of fun, but a loving, protective, solid, never-changing, never-abandoning, and never-abusing Father. He will meet that core void and leave you awestruck by filling it in a way you didn't think was possible. It will change your perception.

There will be times when it may feel like you are a chopped-up onion, going from a hot skillet to a broiling oven. The temperatures can heat up at times to what you may believe are unbearable extremes. He will always meet you there.

> *When you pass through the waters, I will be
> with you*; and when you pass through the
> rivers, they will not sweep over you. *When
> you walk through the fire, you will not be
> burned*; the flames will not set you ablaze.
> (Isaiah 43:2, emphasis added)

Your life will not be the same because you are not the same. You have been transformed. You went through the wilderness and didn't die in it. No! You now flourish because you released the weights that slowed you down for too long. Everything within you that caused you to function in such a fragmented state is in a renewal process because you are submitted and committed. As you align yourself with the heart of a God who is unconditionally and forever rooting for your good, your heart becomes one with his own, and you walk with him as one.

The single heart.

This is what the Sovereign LORD says: On the day I cleanse you from all your sins, I will resettle your towns, and the ruins will be rebuilt. The desolate land will be cultivated instead of lying desolate in the sight of all who pass through it. They will say, "This land that was laid waste has become like the Garden of Eden; the cities that were lying in ruins, desolate and destroyed, are now fortified and inhabited." Then the nations around you that remain will know that I the LORD have rebuilt what was destroyed and have replanted what was desolate. I the LORD have spoken, and I will do it.

—EZEKIEL 36:33–36

Notes

- Chapter 2: Right Thinking, CDC National Health Report Highlights, Centers for Disease Control and Prevention, last modified November 17, 2014, https://www.cdc.gov/healthreport/publications/compendium.pdf

- Chapter 2: Right Thinking, "How Many Cells Are in the Human Body? Fast Facts", Healthline, Suzanne Falck, MD, last modified July 16, 2018, https://www.healthline.com/health/number-of-cells-in-body#types-of-cells

- Chapter 2: Right Thinking, "How Many Cells Are in the Human Body", Medical News Today, Yella Hewings-Martin PHD, last modified July 12, 2017, https://www.medicalnewstoday.com/articles/318342.php

- Chapter 2: Right Thinking, Metcalf, Thomas. "The Self Improvement Industry" accessed February 21, 2019. http://smallbusiness.chron.com/self-improvement-industry-76125.html

- Chapter 2: Right Thinking, "What Does It Mean to Have a Sound Mind?", Rick Renner, last modified February 6, 2017, https://renner.org/what-does-it-mean-to-have-a-sound-mind/

- Chapter 4: Effects of Broken Relationships, "How Divorce Affects Children", Emery on Divorce, http://www.emeryondivorce.com/how_divorce_affects_children.php

- Chapter 4: Effects of Broken Relationships, "32 Shocking Divorce Statistics", McKinley Irvin, last modified October 30, 2012, https://www.mckinleyirvin.com/family-law-blog/2012/october/32-shocking-divorce-statistics/

- Chapter 6: Hidden things, Covenant Eyes, last modified 2019, https://www.covenanteyes.com

- Chapter 6: Hidden Things, "11 Facts About Sex Trafficking", Do Something.Org, https://www.dosomething.org/us/facts/11-facts-about-human-trafficking

- Chapter 7: Sex, Desire, and Abstinence, "Premarital Sex Is Nearly Universal Among Americans, and Has Been For Decades", Guttmacher Institute, last modified December 19, 2006, https://www.guttmacher.org/news-release/2006/premarital-sex-nearly-universal-among-americans-and-has-been-decades

- Chapter 8: The Better Half Myth, "My better half"—the meaning and origin of this phrase, Gary Martin, https://www.phrases.org.uk/meanings/my-better-half.html

Printed in the United States
By Bookmasters